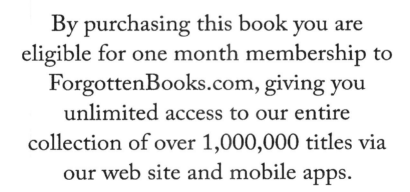

ISBN 978-0-260-19235-6
PIBN 10933494

This book is a reproduction of an important historical work. Forgotten Books uses
state-of-the-art technology to digitally reconstruct the work, preserving the original format
whilst repairing imperfections present in the aged copy. In rare cases, an imperfection in
the original, such as a blemish or missing page, may be replicated in our edition. We do,
however, repair the vast majority of imperfections successfully; any imperfections that
remain are intentionally left to preserve the state of such historical works.

LIST OF WORKS RELATING TO
CITY WASTES AND STREET HYGIENE

NEW YORK

1912

LIST OF WORKS ON CITY WASTES AND STREET HYGIENE
IN THE NEW YORK PUBLIC LIBRARY

BIBLIOGRAPHY

See also below the General Works under date of 1899.

Carnegie Library of Pittsburgh. Refuse and garbage disposal. References to books and magazine articles. Pittsburgh, 1909. 39 p. 8°.

Technique, La, sanitaire. **SPA**
Includes an "Index Bibliographique" arranged by subjects. The division "Immondices" is very full.

GENERAL WORKS

Serial

American Public Health Association. Report of the committee on the disposal of garbage and refuse. Rudolph Hering, chrm. **SPA**

1895. Journal Amer. Public Health Assoc. v. 20, p. 196–202.
1893. Journal Amer. Public Health Assoc. v. 22 p. 105–108.
1897. Public health. v. 23, p. 206–218.
1898–1899. Omitted.
1900. Public health. v. 26, p. 126–129.
1901. Public health. v. 27, p.184–185.
1902. Public health. v. 28, p. 21–28.
1903. Public health. v. 29, p. 129–133.

American Society of Municipal Improvements. Report of committee on disposition of garbage and [on] street cleaning, 1897-1911. **SERA**
Published as part of the Proceedings of the society. The committee has not made a report every year.

Annual Institute of Cleansing Superintendents [of Scotland]. **SPA**
The proceedings are published in the County and municipal record.

Fortschritte der Strassenhygiene. Hrgbn. von Dr. Th. Weyl, Jena, 1901. Heft 1. 8°. **† VDH**
No more issued.

Kommunales Jahrbuch. Jahrg. 1-4. 1908-1911/12. **SERA**
One division of the book, viz. "Städtereinigung," comprises an annual survey of progress as to street cleaning and refuse removal in German cities.

Municipal year book of the United Kingdom. **SER**
Published annually since 1897. Contains a list of British cities showing for each the method of refuse disposal. Refuse removal was not separately featured until about 1905 or 1906.

United States. Census Bureau. Special reports. Statistics of cities, 1902/3-1908. **† SDN**
1902/3 and 1904 were published as Bulletins 20 and 50 resp. of the Bureau. 1902/3 contains no material relative to garbage removal or to street cleaning separately classified. Beginning with 1904 each volume contains tables of receipts and expenditures resp. for each city, over 30,000 population, on account of garbage removal, street cleaning and snow and ice removal. The volumes for 1905, 1906 and 1907 show in addition the number of men employed, equipment, area cleaned and sprinkled, and the quantity and kind of garbage and sweepings collected and disposed of. The volume for 1908 is the last volume issued.

Non-serial

1873

Leas, C. A. Report upon the sanitary care and utilization of the refuse of cities. (American Public Health Assoc. Public health papers and reports. v. 1, p. 454-458.) **SPA**

1878

Ames, Azel. Removal and utilization of domestic excreta. (American Public Health Assoc. Public health papers and reports. v. 4, p. 65-80.) **SPA**

1879

Vallin, E. De la désinfection par les poussières sèches. (Revue d'hygiène et de police sanitaire. v. 1, p. 43-59; 106-117.) **SPA**

1881

Vallin, E. De l'emploi des sels deliquescents pour l'arrosage des voies publiques. (Revue d'hygiène et de police sanitaire. v. 3, p. 600-607.) **SPA**

1882

Keating, J. M. The cremation of excreta and household refuse. (American Public Health Assoc. Public health papers and reports. v. 8, p. 150-154.) **SPA**

1883

Virchow, R. Ueber Städtereinigung und die Verwendung der städtischen Unreinigkeiten. (Vierteljahrsschrift für offentliche Gesundheitspflege. v. 15, p. 583-618.) **SPA**

1884

Du Mesnil, O. Nettoiement de la voie publique; enlèvement des ordures ménagères, leur utilisation. (Annales d'hygiène publique. ser. 3, v. 12, p. 305-327.) **SPA**
Methods in vogue in Lille, Havre, Lyon, Marseille, Bordeaux, Bruxelles, Amsterdam, Rome, Londres, Berlin, Dresde, Munich.

General Works, cont'd.

Profit in street refuse. (The American architect and building news. v. 15, p. 273-274.) **MQA**

Scott, W. B. Cleansing streets and ways in the metropolis and large cities. (International Health Exhibition. The health exhibition literature. London, 1884. 8°. v. 7, p. 389-496.) **SPI**

1885

Eassie, W. On the collection and disposal of house refuse. (Journal Sanitary Institute. v. 6, p. 223-229.) **SPA**

Garbage cremator. 300 w., 4 drawings. (Sanitary engineer. v. 11, p. 170.) †† **VDA**
Concise description of cremator used by the U. S. Sanitary and Fertilizer Co.

—— Same. 250 w., 2 drawings. (Same. v. 11, p. 253.) †† **VDA**
Bee-hive type.

White, W. Howard. European sewage and garbage removal. (Transactions. American Society of Civil Engineers. v. 15, p. 847-872, 4 diagr.) **VDA**

—— Same, extract. (American architect and building news. v. 21, p. 197-198.) **MQA**

1886

Du Mesnil, O. De l'enlèvement et du transport des immondices et des ordures ménagères. (Revue d'hygiène et de police sanitaire. v. 8, p. 560-572. illus.) **SPA**
With table and chart showing resp. the cost and quantity of waste and dirt removed from Paris each year, 1868 to 1884.

McMillan, Walter G. On some appliances for the utilisation of refuse and dust fuel. (Journal of Society of Arts. v. 34, p. 527-541.) **VA**

Zellweger, John. Cremation of garbage. 1000 w., 6 drawings. (Journal and Trans. of Assoc. of Engineering Societies. v. 5, p. 255.) **VDA**

—— Same. (Scientific American supplement. v. 22, p. 8785.) †† **VA**

1888

Codrington, Thomas. Destruction of town refuse. 6500 w., 14 drawings. (Engineering and building record. v. 18, p. 184, 196, 232, 245; v. 19, p. 51.) †† **VDA**
British practice in refuse incineration as carried out in Manchester, Birmingham, Blackpool, Glasgow, Leeds and Bolton.

Garbage cremation. Science. v. 12, p. 265-266.) **OA**
Methods.

Kilvington, S. S. Garbage furnaces and the destruction of organic matter by fire. (American Public Health Assoc. Public health papers and reports. v. 14, p. 156-170, illus.) **SPA**

—— Same, condensed. (Engineering and building record. v. 19, p. 159.) †† **VDA**
Furnaces in use in England and America compared from the point of view of efficiency and economy.

Sweet, W. A. Destruction of town refuse. 250 w. (Engineering and building record. v. 18, p. 210.) †† **VDA**
Author describes his design similar to a blast furnace.

1889

Du Mesnil, O., and JOURNET. De l'enlèvement et de l'utilisation des détritus solides (fumiers, boues, gadoues, débris de cuisine, etc.) dans les villes et les campagnes. (Congrès International d'Hygiène et de Démographie, 1889. p. 254-303.) **SPA**

189–?

Pennsylvania. Health Board. Regulations for the storage and removal of garbage. Recommended for adoption by boards of health in cities and boroughs. n. p. [189–?] 6 p. 8°. (Circular 43.) **SPB**

1890

Drouineau, G. Des dépots ruraux ou agricoles d'immondices. (Revue d'hygiène et de police sanitaire. v. 12, p. 609-627.) **SPA**

Four Whiting pour la carbonisation des ordures ménagères. 250 w., 2 drawings. (Le génie civil. v. 16, p. 431.) †† **VA**

Gerloisy, Sigismund von. Recherches sur la désinfection pratique des matières usées. (Revue d'hygiène et de police sanitaire. v. 12, p. 128-139.) **SPA**

Transport des immondices des villes par chemins de fer. (Same. v. 12, p. 650-654.) **SPA**

1891

Disposal of refuse in American cities. 900 w. (Engineering news. v. 26, p. 51.) †† **VDA**
Brief summary of methods used in 10 largest American cities; based on report by W. V. Hayt, general sanitary officer Chicago Health Dept.

Foster, Wolcott C. Disposal of town refuse and garbage. 2500 w., 3 drawings. (Engineering. v. 52, p. 720.) †† **VDA**

Household refuse. 2000 w. (Same. v. 51, p. 590.) †† **VDA**
Editorial discussion and suggestions for its disposal and utilization as carried on by a London company.

Jones, Charles. The refuse destructor. (Transactions 7th International Congress of Hygiene and Demography. v. 7, p. 189-203.) **SPA**

Weyl, Th. On the cleansing of the streets and the removal of household refuse in German towns. (Same. v. 7, p. 203-204.) **SPA**

General Works, cont'd.

1892

Cockrill, John W. Use of sea-water for street watering, sewer flushing, and the other purposes required by sanitary authorities. (Minutes of Proc. of the Institution of Civil Engineers. v. 110, p. 343-354.)
VDA

Jones, Charles. Disposal of house and town refuse. (Transactions Sanitary Institute. v. 13, p. 44-51.)
SPA

Parsons. Report on an inquiry concerning the nuisances arising during the transport of manure from towns to agricultural districts, and the means available for their prevention or mitigation. (Great Britain Medical Department. Annual report 1891-/2. p. 79-124.)
SPC

Refuse cremators. 10,000 w., 6 drawings (Engineering record. v. 26, p. 297, 312, 328, 397; v. 27, p. 379.)
†† VDA
Working of different types in England and America; Engle, Merz and Rider furnaces given as principal American types.

Russell, Joseph. House dust refuse. (Transactions Sanitary Institute. v. 13, p. 52-58.)
SPA

Simonin, I. M. Sanitary treatment of garbage and infected materials by the "Simonin Process." (American Public Health Assoc. Papers and reports. v. 18, p. 405-408.)
SPA

—— Sanitary utilization of garbage and refuse, and destruction of germ-life in infected material without injury to article treated. 1400 w. (Annals of hygiene. v. 7, p. 339.)
SPA

Watson, George. Disposal of refuse. 6500 w., 3 drawings. (Engineering. v. 54, p. 369, 430.)
†† VDA

—— Same. (Engineering news. v. 28, p. 319, 522.)
†† VDA

—— Same, abstract. 1500 w. (Report British Assoc. for Advancement of Science. v. 62, p. 860.)
*EC
Describes Fryer, Warner, Whiley and Horsfall furnaces as showing most promise in British practice.

Weyl, Th. La destruction et la mise en valeur des gadoues et ordures urbaines en Angleterre. (Annales d'Hygiène publique. ser. 3, v. 29, p. 302-303.)
SPA
Review of a paper published in Berliner Klinische Wochenschift. No. 3, 1892.

1893

Cremating garbage. (The American architect and building news. v. 39, p. 155-156.)
MQA

Engle system of garbage cremation. 1000 w. (Engineering news. v. 29, p. 268.)
†† VDA

Roechling, H. Alfred. Der gegenwärtige Stand der Verbrennung des Hausmülls in englischen Städten. (Gesundheitsingenieur. 1893, no. 19.)
SPA

—— Same. (Revue d'hygiène et de police sanitaire. v. 15, p. 929-932.)
SPA

Terne, Bruno. The utilization of garbage. (Journal Franklin Institute. v. 136, p. 221-230.)
VA

—— Same, extract. (American architect and building news. v. 41, p. 185-186.)
MQA
Advocates utilisation of garbage for agricultural purposes after extraction of grease.

1894

Anderson process of garbage cremation. 1200 w., 2 drawings. (Engineering record. v. 30, p. 26-27.)

Anderson system of garbage cremation. 1500 w., 2 illus. (Engineering news, v. 31, p. 380-381.)

Baker, Tom W. Utilisation of town refuse for generating steam. 5000 w., 4 drawings. (Transactions of Society of Engineers. v. 34, p. 183.)
VDA

—— Same. (Cassier's magazine. v. 7, p. 383-391.)
VDA

—— Same. (Engineer, London. v. 78, p. 390.)
†† VDA

Bayless, Charles T., and A. E. Merkel. Garbage cremation in America. 5000 w., 3 drawings. (Engineering news. v. 32, p. 167.)
†† VDA
Reviews successful systems and describes typical furnaces, the Rider furnace at Allegheny, the Merz system at Buffalo and the Engle crematory at the World's Columbian Exposition at Chicago.

Déstruction, La, ambulante des ordures ménagères. (Le génie civil. Année 25, p. 70.)
†† VA

Effère. Combustion des gadoues en Amérique. (Same. Année 25, p. 363-366.)
†† VA
Plants at Governor's Is., Allegheny, Merz process and Engle cremator.

McKay, The, Garbage cremator. (Engineering record. v. 31, p. 57.)
VDA

Merz system of garbage utilization in four American cities. 8000 w., 9 drawings, 4 illus. (Same. v. 32, p. 354.)
†† VDA
Describes plants at St. Louis, Buffalo, Milwaukee and Detroit.

Regenerative garbage cremators. 1200 w., 1 drawing. (Engineering record. v. 30, p. 110.)
†† VDA

Schneider, Richard. Aufarbeitung von gewerblichen und häuslichen Abfallstoffen. (Congrès International d'Hygiène et de Démographie. 8 session, 1894. Compte rendu. v. 5, p. 403-406.)
SPA

—— Same, review. (Revue d'hygiène et de police sanitaire. v. 16, p. 914-915.)
SPA

Weyl, Theodor. Studien zur Strassenhygiene mit besonderer Berücksichtigung der Müllverbrennung. Jena: G. Fischer, 1893. viii, 142 p., illus., 11 folding plates. 8°.
VDH

General Works, cont'd.

—— Same, review. (Centralblatt für die allgemeine Gesundheitspflege. v. 13, p. 310-315.) **SPA**
Dr. Weyl accompanied the director of the street cleaning system of Berlin on a tour of the continental cities in 1891, which furnished the material for the present volume, which is confined to the cities of Brussels, Paris and London.

1895

Appareils de combustion des gadoues. 2400 w., 4 drawings, 1 foldg. plate. (Le génie civil. v. 26, p. 231.) **†† VA**
Description of the Merz reduction system and of the Thackeray and Mackay furnaces in American cities.

Combustion des ordures ménagères et des gadoues des rues; le four Horsfall. 1400 w., 2 drawings. (Same. v. 27, p. 415.) **†† VA**
Brief descriptions of the Fryer, Warner, Whiley and Horsfall furnaces.

Deas, James. On the disposal of town and other refuse by burning. (Journal Sanitary Institute. v. 16, p. 17-19.) **SPA**

Dunne, George. The destruction of house refuse by burning. (Sanitary journal. n. s., v. 2, p. 264-269.) **SPA**

McKenzie, T. H. Remarks on disposal of garbage and household refuse. (American Public Health Assoc. Journal. v. 20, p. 184-186.) **SPA**

Mason, Charles. Scavenging. Disposal of refuse. (Journal Sanitary Institute. v. 16, p. 464-481.) **SPA**

Royle, H. On the Acme refuse destructor. (Same. v. 16, p. 20-22.) **SPA**

Wordin, N. E. The disposal of domestic garbage. (American Public Health Assoc. Journal. v. 20, p. 178-183.) **SPA**

1896

Abell, William Price. Megass and refuse furnaces. (Cassier's magazine. v. 10, p. 192-196; illus.) **VDA**

—— Same. Minutes of Proc. of Institution of Civil Engineers. v. 123, p. 369-376.) **VDA**

Fuertes, James H. Garbage disposal in England. 2200 w. (Engineering news. v. 36, p. 10.) **†† VDA**
Results obtained at Leeds, Liverpool, Cambridge, etc.

—— Garbage cremation in Europe. 2300 w. (Engineering record. v. 34, p. 102.) **†† VDA**
Observation of plants at Hamburg, Leeds and Cambridge.

Garbage cremation in Germany. 4500 w. (Same. v. 34, p. 45.) **†† VDA**
Letter from Rudolph Hering giving letters from German engineers regarding plants at Hamburg and Berlin.

Johnson garbage crematory. 1000 w., 2 drawings. (Engineering news. v. 35, p. 86.) **†† VDA**

Orme, H. S. Street cleaning and disposal of garbage. (California. Health Board. 14 bienn. report, 1894/6, p. 182-189.) **SPB**
Operations in certain California and other American cities.

1897

Adam, C. Vorschläge zur Verbesserung der Abfuhr des Hausunraths in Städten. (Centralblatt für allgemeine Gesundheitspflege. v. 16, p. 293-300.) **SPA**

Büsing, F. W. Die Städtereinigung. [Heft 1.] Stuttgart, 1897. 342 p., 14 illus. 8°. **SPA**
The volume itself is not, at this time, in the Library. It is reviewed in Deutsche Vierteljahrsschrift für öffentliche Gesundheitspflege. v. 29, p. 595. The second part was published in 1901; see below that date.

Chiapponi, N. Sull' eliminazione e sull' utilizzamento delle spazzature nelle grandi città. Relazione letta alla Reale Società Italiana d'Igiene. (Giornale della Reale Società Italiana d' Igiene. v. 19, p. 10-18; 45-51; p. 79-87; 97-110. illus.) **SPA**

Hering, Rudolph. Vexed question of garbage disposal. 2800 w., 1 diagr. (Engineering magazine. v. 13, p. 392.) **VDA**
Methods in use and their relative advantages.

Kehricht-Verbrennung in England. (Centralblatt für allgemeine Gesundheitspflege. v. 16, p. 301-310.) **SPA**
Report by Stadtbaurath Wiebe of Essen as chairman of a commission sent by the city of Essen to inspect English refuse destruction plants.

Meyer, Andreas. Ueber den Stand der Kehrichtverbrennung in Deutschland. (Same. v. 17, p. 259-268.) **SPA**
Paper read at the 22d session of the Deutscher Verein für öffentliche Gesundheitspflege, Karlsruhe, Sept. 14-17, 1877.

Morse-Boulger garbage and refuse destructor. 1000 w. (Engineering record. v. 35, p. 520.) **†† VDA**

Schiff für Mülltransport. (Gesundheits-Ingenieur. Jahrg. 20, p. 39, illus.) **†† SPA**

Unsatisfactory conditions of garbage disposal in America. 1200 w. (Engineering news. v. 38, p. 313.) **†† VDA**
Editorial discussion and commendation of the report of the committee on garbage disposal of the American Public Health Assoc.

Vallin, E. La destruction et l'utilisation agricole des immondices urbaines. (Revue d'hygiène et de police sanitaire. v. 19, p. 693-708.) **SPA**

Vogel, J. H. Die Beseitigung und Verwertung des Hausmülls vom hygienischen und volkswirtschaftlichen Standpunkte. Jena: Gustav Fischer 1897. 6, 68 p. 8°. 17 illus., 1 plan. **VDI**

General Works, cont'd.

—— Same, review. Centralblatt für die allgemeine Gesundheitspflege. v. 16, p. 505-507.) **SPA**

Warden-Stevens, F. J. Electric supply and the destruction of town refuse. 2800 w. (Architect and contract reporter. v. 57, p. 315.) **† MQA**

Watson, W. M. Disposal of towns' refuse. 10,000 w., 10 drawings. (Canadian engineer. v. 5, p. 218, 250, 286, 313.) **VDA**

Wordin, N. E. A plea for the domestic disposal of garbage. 3000 w. (Journal American Public Health Assoc. Jan. 1897, p. 79.) **SPA**
Relates to American cities only.

1898

Cremation of dust-bin refuse. 3000 w. (Engineering. v. 65, p. 179, 212.) **†† VDA**

Disposal of waste liquids from garbage reduction. 700 w. (Engineering record. v. 37, p. 490.) **†† VDA**

Gerhard, W. P. Über Müll- und Abfallverbrennung im Hause. (Gesundheits-Ingenieur. Jahrg. 21, p. 259-260, illus.) **†† SPA**

Haefcke. Die Beseitigung und Verwertung von Fleischabfällen und tierischen Kadavern. (Same. Jahrg. 21, p. 332-333.) **†† SPA**

Häntzschel, Walther. Die Beseitigung des Hausmülls (System Kinsbruner). (Same. Jahrg. 21, p. 329-332, illus.) **†† SPA**

Horsfall induced draught system. 600 w., 3 drawings. (Engineer, London. v. 86, p. 40.) **†† VDA**

Macfarlane, Thomas. Remarks on the disposal of refuse in some European cities. (American Public Health Assoc. Public health papers and reports. v. 24, p. 31-50.) **SPA**
London, Leyton, Walthamstowe, Berlin, Birmingham, Manchester, Oldham, Rochdale, Glasgow, Hawick, Leipzig, Freiberg, Bremen, Braunschweig.

Ridley, A. E. Brooke. Garbage destructors. 900 w., 1 drawing, 2 illus. (Electricity. v. 14, p. 277.) **†† VGA**
Three principal systems of refuse destruction and heat utilization as used at Shoreditch, Ealing and Oldham.

Veeder, M. A., and J. L. Richards. Garbage reduction by steam. (American Public Health Assoc. Public health papers and reports. v. 24, p. 296-299.) **SPA**

Waring, George E., jr. Street-cleaning and the disposal of a city's wastes: methods and results and the effect upon public health, public morals, and municipal prosperity. New York: Doubleday & McClure Co., 1898. 5 p.l., 230 p., 2 pl., 1 port. 12°. **VDH**

Weyl, Theodor. Experimentelles und kritisches über Schneebeseitigung. (Gesundheits-Ingenieur. Jahrg. 21, p. 381-383.) **†† SPA**

1899

Campbell, A. H. Synopsis of paper reviewing some of the English attempts to utilize heat from garbage crematories for producing electric light current. (Municipal engineering. v. 17, p. 99.) **VDA**

Coigne, Edmond. Assainissement des villes. Dessication et transformation des matières putrescibles, sang, viandes, matières épaisses de vidanges, gadoues, ordures ménagères. (Le génie civil. v. 6, p. 12-15, 23-24, 39-41; illus.) **†† VA**
Methods of destruction and their applicability to Paris.

Craven, MacDonough. Waste disposal and its advances. (American Public Health Assoc. Public health papers and reports. v. 25, p. 293-311.) **SPA**

English experience with garbage as fuel for electric light stations. 600 w. (Engineering news. v. 42, p. 21.) **†† VDA**

Kelvin, Lord, and Archibald Barr. Horsefall destructor. 1,500 w., 2 drawings. (Engineering, London. v. 87, p. 260.) **†† VDA**
Abstract of report after inspection of plants at Edinburgh, Bradford and Oldham.

Koller, Theodor. Erfahrungen in der städtischen Hausmüllverwerthung. (Annalen für Gewerbe u. Bauwesen. 1899, p. 252-254.) **VDA**

—— Same, review. (Minutes of Proc. of Institution of Civil Engineers. v. 138, p. 508-509.) **VDA**
Review of results of English and German practice in garbage cremation, especially in Munich. Utilization of resulting products.

Morse, William F. The next step in the work of refuse and garbage disposal. (American Public Health Assoc. Public health papers and reports. v. 25, p. 312-332.) **SPA**
Progress in American and continental cities.

—— Utilization of city refuse. 1000 w., 1 illus. (Municipal engineering. v. 16, p. 303.) **VDA**
Success in utilizing heat from refuse cremation.

Municipal cremation of garbage. 400 w. (Engineering and building record. v. 20, p. 356.) **†† VDA**
Bibliography of material to 1889 in "Sanitary engineer" and "Engineering and building record."

Reynolds, Arthur R. Garbage disposal. (Municipal engineering. v. 16, p. 31-33.) **VDA**

Über Strassenwaschmaschinen. (Gesundheits-Ingenieur. Jahrg. 22, p. 403-404.) **†† SPA**

General Works, cont'd.

United States. Animal Industry Bureau. Disposition of dead animals in foreign cities. (16 Annual Report. 1899, p. 346-361.)   **VPO**

London, Dublin, Paris, Berlin, Vienna, Brussels, Stockholm, Amsterdam. Material relates to economic as well as sanitary disposal.

Watson, George. Refuse furnaces. (Minutes and Proc. Institution of Civil Engineers. v. 135, p. 300-319.)   **VDA**

Weyl, Theodor. Über Strassenwaschmaschinen. (Gesundheits-Ingenieur. Jahrg. 22, p. 253-255.)   †† **SPA**

1900

Congrès International d'Hygiène et de Démographie, 10. 1900, Paris.   **SPA**

The proceedings themselves are not, at this time, in the Library. Abstracts of papers relating to refuse disposal read at the congress are in the Library as follows:

HUDELO. Les ordures ménagères, leur collecte, leur transport et leur traitement final; règles hygiéniques à suivre dans les maisons et dans les villes. (Annales d'Hygiène Publique. ser. 3, v. 44, p. 333-334.) SPA
—— Same. (Revue d'hygiène et de police sanitaire. v. 22, p. 1006-1007.)   SPA
TRELAT, E. Conditions imposées par l'hygiène aux reglements de voire dans les agglomérations urbaines. (Revue d'hygiène et de police sanitaire. v. 22, p. 1010-1011.)   SPA
WEYL, Th. Principes concernant l'hygiène des rues. (Annales d'hygiène publique. ser. 3, v. 44, p. 333-334.)   SPA

Erismann, Th. Combustion et désinfection des ordures des habitations et des rues. (Revue d'hygiène publique et de police sanitaire. v. 23, p. 633-635.)   **SPA**

Review of article in Archives russes de pathologie, de médecine clinique, etc. v. 9, p. 441 et seq.

Healey, Brierly Denham. Economical disposal of town refuse. 8300 w., 14 drawings. (Transactions Soc. of Engineers. v. 40, p. 65.)   **VDA**

—— Same, abstract. 1600 w. (Engineer, London. v. 90, p. 192.)   †† **VDA**

Costs in detail and economical methods of utilizing heated gases.

Kittilsen, Edward. An efficient system of garbage collection for a small city. (Municipal engineering. v. 18, p. 160-162.)   **VDA**

Koeppen, Gustav. Müllverbrennungsversuche nach Dörr'schem System. (Centrallblatt für allgemeine Gesundheitspflege. Jahrg. 22, p. 67-69. [Review.])   **SPA**

Kori, H. Verbrennungsöfen für Abfälle. (Gesundheits-Ingenieur. Jahrg. 23, p. 396-398. illus.)   **SPA**

Relates particularly to institutional incinerators.

Livache, Achille. Considérations sur les divers modes de traitement des ordures ménagères. 7000 w. (Bulletin de la Société d'Encouragement pour l'Industrie Nationale. v. 99, p. 730-748.)   **VA**

—— Same, condensed. (Revue d'hygiène et de police sanitaire. v. 22, p. 949-951.)   **SPA**

Reviews especially American and British practice of refuse disposal.

Modified Horsfall crematory. 700 w., 7 drawings. (Engineering record. v. 41, p. 111.)   †† **VDA**

Pagliani, L. Incinerazione delle immondizie delle case e delle strade. Forni "Horsfall." (Revue d'hygiène et de police sanitaire. v. 22, p. 951-952.)   **SPA**

This is a review of the original article which appeared in L'Ingegnere Ingienista 1900, p. 187, 200. This journal is not in the Library.

Scherer, H. P. How properly to collect and dispose of garbage. (Municipal engineering. v. 19, p. 331-335.)   **VDA**

Segundo, Ed. C. de. Disposal of town's refuse. 1200 w. (Electrical review, London. v. 47, p. 451.)   †† **VGA**

Comment on McTaggart's paper; see below Special Cities (Bradford).

—— Refuse and its calorific power. 1700 w. (Same, London. v. 46, p. 41.)   †† **VGA**

Comment on Russell's paper of 1899; see below Special Cities (London).

Smith, E. Shrapnell. Working costs of automobiles for street watering and dust removal. (Automotor journal. v. 4, p. 628-629.)   † **TOL**

—— Same, review. (Minutes of Proc. of Institution for Civil Engineers. v. 144, p. 409-410.)   **VDA**

Société de Médecine Publique. Sur la destruction des ordures ménagères. [Discussion by Messrs. Vincey and Livache.] (Revue d'hygiène et de police sanitaire. v. 22, p. 448-453.)   **SPA**

Towns' refuse problem. 4000 w. (Electrical review, London. v. 46, p. 945, 957.)   †† **VGA**

Fluctuating calorific value according to season. Refers to Healey's paper.

1901

Baker, M. N. Condition of garbage disposal in United States. (Municipal journal and engineer. v. 11, p. 147-148.)   †† **SERA**

—— Same. (Engineering news. v. 46, p. 116-117.)   †† **VDA**

Büsing, F. W. Die Städtereinigung. Heft 2. Technische Einrichtungen der Städtereinigung. Stuttgart, 1901. iv, (1), 345-865 p. illus. 4°. (Der Städtische Tiefbau, v. 3.)   † **VDH**

Only a very small portion, viz. p. 861-865, relates to refuse disposal. The first part was published in 1897; see above that date.

Goodrich, W. Francis. The economic disposal of towns' refuse. London: P. S. King and Son, 1901. xvi, 340 p. 8°.   **VDI**

—— Town refuse disposal in Great Britain. (Cassier's magazine. v. 21, p. 99-122; illus.)   **VDA**

Cuts of Fryer destructor at Cambridge, Warner destructor at West Hartlepool, Baker destructor of Clerkenwell vestry, Meldrum destructor at Nelson,

General Works, cont'd.

Horsfall destructor at Fulham, Heenan and Froade, destructor at Blackburn, Beaman and Deas destructor at Colne.

Hedenberg, W. L. Garbage as fuel for steam production. (Municipal engineering. v. 20, p. 140-142.)   **VDA**

Highfield, J. S. Refuse destructors in combination with electric power stations 2200 w.; discussion on 4000 w. (Electrician, London. v. 47, p. 606.)   **†† VGA**

—— Same. (Electrical engineer, London. v. 34, p. 11.)   **†† VGA**

—— Same, condensed. 1800 w. (Electrical review, London. v. 49, p. 120.)   **†† VGA**

Scavenging districts. ₁Organisation in counties of Scotland.₁ (Sanitary journal. n. s., v. 7, p. 580-591.)   **SPA**

Weyl, Theodor. Bemerkungen über den Stand der Müllbeseitigung, mit besonderer Rücksicht auf die Sortieranstalten. (Fortschritte der Strassenhygiene. Heft 1, p. 59-66.)   **† VDH**

—— Der Müllverbrennungsofen von Dr. Dörr. (Same. Heft 1, p. 75-81.)   **† VDH**

—— Die Strassenreinigungsmaschine "Salus." (Same. Heft 1, p. 44-50; illus.)   **† VDH**

1902

Balayeuse—arroseuse—ramasseuse. (Le génie civil. Année 42, p. 80-82; illus.)   **†† VA**

Bertarelli, E. La raccolta e l' utilizzazione delle immondizie stradali e domestiche con particolare riguardo all' igiene pubblica. (Giornale della Reale Società Italiana d' Igiene. v. 24, p. 146-147; review.)   **SPA**

British, A, refuse lighting plant. (Electrical world and engineer. v. 39, p. 725-727.)   **†† VGA**

Broadbent, Frank. Refuse destruction; its sanitary and its steam raising aspects. 10,000 w. 2 diagr., 7 drawings. (Electrical review, London. v. 50, p. 884, 1000; v. 51, p. 174, 92, 334, 529.)

Disposal of garbage in the U. S. (Municipal engineering. v. 22, p. 395-397.)   **VDA**

With list showing garbage reduction and cremation plants in places of 30,000 population.

État actuel de la question des ordures ménagères dans les divers pays. 15000 w., 12 drawings. (Bulletin de la Société d'encouragement pour l'industrie nationale. v. 102, p. 178.)   **VA**

Review of practice in refuse disposal in all parts of the world based on Goodrich's "Economic disposal of towns' refuse."

Gibson, John. How the individual citizen might cooperate in the cleaning of a town or city. (Municipal record and sanitary journal. v. 1, p. 425-431.)   **SPA**

Read at a congress of the Association of Cleansing Superintendents, held at Edinburgh in July, 1902.

Goodrich, W. Francis. Electricity from refuse; the case for the modern destructor. 4200 w.; discussion 1200 w., 2 drawings. (Electrician, London. v. 50, p. 220.)

—— Same, condensed. 3800 w. (Electrical engineer, London. v. 36, Nov. 14 suppl., p. 5.)

—— Same, condensed. 1200 w. (Electrical review, London. v. 51, p. 851.)

Hamblett, W. H. The disposal of towns' refuse. (Journal Sanitary Institute. v. 23, p. 775-781.)   **SPA**

Hygiène des voies publiques. (Revue d'hygiène publique et de police sanitaire. v. 25, p. 825-829.)   **SPA**

Abstract of the report of the International Committee on road hygiene. The committee was composed of H. A. Roechling (Berne), president, Dr. F. Schmid (Berne), Dr. Bohm (Berlin), Dr. J. Polak (Warsaw), Prof. L. Pagliani (Turin) and Prof. Tedeschi (Turin).

Kern, Emile. Le traitement des ordures ménagères. (Same. v. 24, p. 326-350; 439-442.)   **SPA**

L., J. La destruction des ordures mènagères. (Le génie civil. v. 41, p. 7-10; illus.)   **†† VA**

Livache, Achille. État actuel de la question des ordures ménagères dans les divers pays. (Bulletin de la Société d'Encouragement pour l'Industrie Nationale. v. 102, sem. 1, p. 178-222; illus.)   **VA**

Ordures, Les, ménagères dans les divers pays. (Annales d'hygiène publique. v. 47, p. 369-374.)   **SPA**

Review of Goodrich, the economic disposal of town's refuse. London, 1901 and Ach. Livache État actuel de la question des ordures ménagères dans les divers pays.

Refuse destructors — report of the Aberdeen deputation. (Municipal record and sanitary journal. v. 1, p. 62-64.)   **SPA**

The deputation was appointed by the Aberdeen Corporation to visit certain destructors in the south of Scotland, viz. those in Govan, Partick, Glasgow, Paisley and Edinburgh. The above is an abstract of the report presented.

Reille, Paul. Les ordures ménagères. Enlèvement, evacuation, utilisation. (Annales d'hygiène publique. v. 48, p. 342-358.)   **SPA**

Winslow, C. E. A., and P. HANSEN. Some statistics of garbage disposal for the larger American cities in 1902. From the biological laboratories of the Mass. Institute of Technology. (American Public Health Assoc. Public health papers and reports. v. 29, p. 141-165.)   **SPA**

With a bibliography and a tabulation of cities showing method of disposal of each sort of garbage. Reviewed in Revue d'hygiène et de police sanitaire. v. 27, p. 562-565.

General Works, cont'd.

1903

Booth, W. H. Fuel value of refuse. 1500 w. (Electrical review. v. 52, p. 245.)
†† **VGA**

Broadbent, Frank. "Fuel" value of town refuse; a rejoinder. 2500 w. (Same. v. 52, p. 130.)
†† **VGA**
Reply to article signed Segundo in Page's magazine, v. .

Hering, Rudolph. Garbage disposal in small cities and villages. 2300 w. (Municipal engineering. v. 24, p. 139.)   **VDA**
Abstract of address before the N. Y. Association of Health Officers.

Horsfall refuse destructor and forced draught system. 1400 w., 1 drawing. (Electrical review. v. 53, p. 168.)   ††**VGA**

Morse, William F. The sanitary disposal of municipal and institutional waste by cremation. (American Public Health Assoc. Public health papers and reports. v. 29, p. 134-140.)   **SPA**

Refuse, The, destructor and refuse disposal. (County and municipal record. v. 1, p. 267-271.)   **SPA**
Relates chiefly to Horsfall plants and shows cuts of district at Hamburg, Edinburgh, Paisley and Moss Side.

Sanitary disposal of municipal refuse. 60 p., 4 drawings. (Transactions of the American Society of Civil Engineers. v. 50, p. 95.)   **VDA**
Informal discussion by members. Review of present American practice and prospects, emphasizing the fact that the problem must be dealt with by the engineer.

Use of destructor in power plants. 3500 w., 3 drawings, 1 illus. (Engineer, Cleveland. v. 40, p. 276.)   **VDA**
Principle types of furnaces in use in England.

Utilisation, The, of destructor clinker. (County and municipal record. v. 2, p. 20.)   **SPA**

Verwendung, Die, des Hausmülls in der Landwirthschaft. (Zeitschrift für Transportwesen und Strassenbau. Jahrg. 22, p. 505-506, 520-521.)   †† **TPB**

Verwendung, Die, von Motorfahrzeugen für städtische Strassenreinigung, Müllbeseitigung etc. in England. (Same. Jahrg. 22, p. 455-456.)   †† **TPB**

1904

Baker, M. N. Refuse destructors. (Bulletin of the League of American Municipalities. v. 2, p. 62-64.)   **SERA**

—— Same. (Municipal engineering. v. 27, p. 447.)   **VDA**
Comparison of British and American practices and methods.

Broadbent, Frank. Combination of dust destructors and electricity works econom-

ically considered. 2700 w., 3 diagr. (Electrical review, London. v. 55, p. 1041.)
†† **VGA**
Criticism of conclusions reached by M. P. Adams.

Brookman, F. W. Power plants. By F. W. Brookman. (County and municipal record. v. 3, p. 265-268, 285-289.)   **SPA**
Includes tables of tests made of Horsfall destructors at Accrington, Oldham and Hereford, Warrington, Rochdale, Blackburn, Cleckheaton, Portglasgow, West Hartlepool, Darwen, Fulham, Wandsworth, Nelson, Plumstead, Liverpool, Partick, Nottingham, Walford, Burnley, Sheerness.

Case, The, for the refuse destructor. (County and municipal record. v. 3, p. 38-39.)   **SPA**
Extract from annual report of Dr. Robertson, medical officer of health for Leith; advocates destruction by burning.

City practices in garbage collection and disposal. (Municipal engineering. v. 26, p. 182.)   **VDA**
Synopsis of report of joint garbage committees of the Council and the Board of Health of Grand Rapids, Mich.

Combination of dust destructors and electricity works economically considered. 44 p., 30 diagr. (Journal Institution of Electrical Engineers. v. 34, p. 256.)   **VGA**

—— Same, condensed. (Electrician, London. v. 54, p. 348, 387, 423, 467, 542.)
†† **VGA**

—— Same, abstract. 1800 w. (Electrical engineer, London. v. 40, p. 925.)   †† **VGA**
Comparative results from all the combined plants in England.

Eccles, W. H. Improvement in townscleansing. (County and municipal record. v. 3, p. 244-246.)   **SPA**

Gent. Personal impressions of a chairman of a cleansing committee. (County and municipal record. v. 3, p. 241-244.)   **SPA**
Paper read at 7th annual congress of Association of Cleansing Superintendents. House refuse, conversions; trade refuse; street sweeping.

Hering, Rudolph. Disposal of municipal refuse; review of general practice. 42 p. (Transactions American Society of Civil Engineers. v. 54, part 5, p. 265.)
VDA
Discussion 27 p. Comprehensive review of American practice of collection and disposal of refuse.

Idström, G. Om sopförbränning. (Tekniska föreningen i Finland. Förhandlingar. Arg. 24, p. 51-54.)   † **VDA**

Massachusetts. Health Board. Report rel. to dumping of garbage and rubbish in harbors and along seacoast of Massachusetts Bay. 27 p. 1 map (Mass. Senate docs. 1907, no. 277.)

Morse, William F. Garbage disposal work in America. (Municipal journal and engineer. v. 17, p. 158-160.)   †† **SER**

—— Utilization and disposal of municipal waste. 8000 w., 11 drawings, 14 illus.

General Works, cont'd.

(Journal of the Franklin Institute.   v. 157, p. 401; v. 158, p. 304.)   **VA**
Review of development in England and the U. S.

Thiesing, Hans.   Müllbeseitigung und Müllverwertung im Jahre 1904.   (Gesundheits-Ingenieur.   Jahrg. 28, p. 60–62.)   **†† SPA**

Tur, P.   Note on the removal and utilization of municipal refuse in French cities. 3700 w.   (Transactions of the American Soc. of Civil Engineers. v. 54, part 5, p. 309.)   **VDA**

——— Same.   (American architect and building news.   v. 86, p. 29-31.)   **MQA**

Watson, George.   The burning of town refuse.   (Engineering.   v. 77, p. 830-835.)   **†† VDA**

——— Same.   (Magazine of commerce. v. 4, p. 431-435.)   **† TLA**

Woodhead, Howard.   Street cleaning in German cities.   (Municipal journal and engineer.   v. 17. p. 97-100.)   **†† SER**

1905

Atkinson, A. S.   Economy of the modern garbage destructor.   (Western electrician garbage destructor.   2500 w.   (Western electrician.   v. 36, p. 236.)   **†† VGA**
Utilization of heat from British destructors.

Bayles, Howard Green.   Incineration of municipal waste.   4000 w.   (Municipal engineering.   v. 29, p. 255.)   **VDA**
Review of cost and efficiency of incineration in various American cities.

Borne, Georges.   Les ordures ménagères: collecte, enlèvement et destruction. (Revue Pratique d'hygiène municipale.   Année 1, p. 529-537.)   **SPA**

Branch, The, garbage incinerator.   (Municipal engineering.   v. 29, p. 140-143; 3 illus.)   **VDA**

British refuse destructors.   4800 w.   (Engineering news.   v. 53, p. 380, 405, 438.)   **†† VDA**

British refuse destructors and American garbage furnaces.   2800 w.   (Same.   v. 53, p. 388.)   **†† VDA**

Englische Anlagen für Hausmüll-Verbrennung in ihren neuesten Konstruktionen.   (Zeitschrift für Transportwesen und Strassenbau.   Jahrg. 22, p. 328-330, 345-346, 362-364; illus.)   **†† TPB**

Functions of a garbage crematory.   700 w.   (Municipal engineering.   v. 29, p. 220.)

Land disposal of garbage; an opportunity for engineers and contractors.   2500 w. (Engineering news.   v. 53, p. 367.)   **†† VDA**
Advocates plowing of garbage into land.

Linde, C. von der.   Müllvernichtung oder Müllverwertung insbesondere das Dreiteilungsystem.   Charlottenburg, 1906.
The volume itself is not in the Library.   A review of it is published in Gesundheits-Ingenieur. Jahrg. 30, p. 383–384.   **SPA**

Morse, William F.   Disposition of municipal refuse.   American conditions illustrated by data from representative cities.   (American Public Health Assoc.   Public health papers and reports.   v. 26, part 1, p. 41-53.)   **SPA**

Qualifications, The, of a cleansing superintendent.   (County and municipal record. v. 4, p. 269-270.)   **SPA**

Refuse destructors.   2000 w., 4 diagr. (Electrical engineer, London.   v. 41, p. 122.)   **VGA**
Tests of Meldrum destructor.

Rhines, J. K.   The disposal of municipal refuse.   (Journal of Assoc. of Engineering Societies.   v. 33, p. 255-269.)   **VDA**

——— Same.   (Bulletin League of American Municipalities.   v. 3, p. 69-76.)   **SERA**
Summary of methods in use.

Sanitary, A, garbage incinerator (i. e., the Decarie cremator).   (Municipal engineering.   v. 29, p. 224-226; 1 illus.)   **VDA**

Schneebeseitigung, Die, in Städten.   (Zeitschrift für Transportwesen und Strassenbau.   Jahrg. 22, p. 165-166.)   **†† TPB**

Some recent garbage crematories.   (Municipal engineering.   v. 29, p. 59-60.)   **VDA**
U. S. army posts at Governor's Island, N. Y., and Fort Leavenworth, Kans., resp.

Thiesing, Hans.   Müllverwertung, insbesondere nach dem Dreiteilungsverfahren. (Gesundheits-Ingenieur.   Jahrg. 29, p. 7-11; 23-26.)   **††SPA**

Transportable und andere kleinere englische Müllverbrennungsanlagen.   (Zeitschrift für Transportwesen und Strassenbau.   Jahrg. 22, p. 626; illus.)   **†† TPB**

Traveling, A, garbage crematory.   (Municipal engineering.   v. 29, p. 228.)   **VDA**

Ueber Schneefegemaschinen.   (Zeitschrift für Transportwesen und Strassenbau. Jahrg. 22, p. 168.)   **†† TPB**
Shows an illustration of the snow removal car used by the Parkersburg Marietta Interurban Rwy. Co.

Walsh, George E.   City refuse as fuel in electric plants.   2800 w.   (American electrician.   v. 17, p. 372.)   **†† VGA**

Wanzer, M. L.   Generating electricity from waste.   1200 w.   (Bulletin of the League of American Municipalities.   v. 4, p. 189.)   **SERA**

Watson, Frank Leslie.   Destructors and their bye-products.   4000 w.   (Electrician, London.   v. 56, p. 271.)   **†† VGA**
Also relative to tests of generation of steam and electricity by destructors.

General Works, cont'd.

1906

Appareil, Un, à recommender ₁pour le transport des ordures ménagères.₁ (La technique sanitaire. v. 1, p. 43.) †† **SPA**

Branch, Joseph G. Garbage incinerators. 1500 w. (Bulletin of the League of American Municipalities. v. 5, p. 1.) **SERA**
Report to the city council of St. Louis.

—— Heat and light from municipal and other waste... With...illustrations. St. Louis: W. H. O'Brien ₁1906.₁ vii, 305 p. f°. **VDH**

Cleansing, The, of towns and cities in Scotland. I. Historical. II. Street cleaning. III. Removal of refuse. IV. Disposal of refuse. V. Utilisation of clinker and other products. (County and municipal record. v. 7, p. 14–16, 42–43, 82–84, 138–140, 298–300.) **SPA**

Dörr, Clemens. Die Beseitigung von Hausmüll. (Zeitschrift für Transportwesen und Strassenbau. Jahrg. 23, p. 491–494, 513–515, 530–532, 553–556, 578–580.)) †† **TPB**

—— Same. (Zeitschrift des oesterreichischen Ingenieur und Architekten Vereins. Jahrg. 58, p. 465–468, 477–580, 495–500.) **VDA**

—— Synopsis of an address at annual meeting of Baltischer Verein von Gas- und Wasserfachmännern in Stettin on garbage disposal in the light of modern progress. (Deutsche Vierteljahrsschrift für öffentliche Gesundheitspflege. v. 39, p. 703–704.) **SPA**

—— Über Müllverbrennung in den Städten. (Journal für Gasbeleuchtung und Wasserversorgung. Jahrg. 49, p. 626–627.) †† **VOA**
Incineration by the Dörr-Schuppmann system.

Harder. Landwirtschaftliche und industriell-gewerbliche Müllverwertung. (Gesundheits-Ingenieur. Jahrg. 29, p. 277–279; 289–291.) †† **SPA**

Hatton, T. Chalkley. Street cleaning and disposition of sweepings. (Municipal engineering. v. 31, p. 374–377.) **VDA**

Lauenstein, Adolph A. W. Die Verpflichtung zur polizeimässigen Strassenreinigung innerhalb der preussischen Stadt- und Landgemeinden. Borna: R. Noske, 1906. viii, 65 p., 1 l. 8°. **VDH** p.v.1, no.5

Parsons, Henry de B. The disposal of municipal refuse. New York: J. Wiley and Sons, 1906. x, 186 p., 4 plans. illus. 8°. **VDI**

—— Same. (American Soc. of Civil Engineers. Proc., papers and discussions. v. 32, p. 288–325.) †† **VDA**
Practically the same though not verbatim duplicate text. Relates almost entirely to New Yorkp City.

Praktischer, Ein, Müllabfuhrwagen mit selbstättiger Kippvorrichtung. (Zeitschrift für Transportwesen und Strassenbau. Jahrg. 23, p. 623–624; illus.) †† **TPB**

Problem of waste disposal. 250 w. (Municipal journal and engineer. v. 33, p. 236.) **SERA**

—— **Refuse** destructors. (County and municipal record. v. 7, p. 13–14.) **SPA**
Review of a paper by Norman Leask read before a meeting of engineering experts in Glasgow. History and summary of types of destructors.

Thiesing, Hans. Müllbeseitigung und Müllverwertung. (Deutsche Vierteljahrsschrift für öffentliche Gesundheitspflege. v. 38, p. 147–173.) **SPA**
Reviewed in Revue d'hygiène publique et de police sanitaire. v. 29, p. 564–565.

—— Müllverwertung, insbesondere nach dem Dreiteilungsverfahren. (Zeitschrift des oesterreichischen Ingenieur und Architekten Vereins. Jahrg. 58, p. 38–46.) **VDA**

—— Same. (Zeitschrift für Transportwesen und Strassenbau. Jahrg. 22, p. 162–164, 182–184, 208–211.) †† **TPB**

—— Same, condensed. (Deutsche Vierteljahrsschrift für öffentliche Gesundheitspflege. v. 39, p. 704–705.) **SPA**

Tur, P. Les ordures ménagères. (Revue d'hygiène et de police sanitaire. v. 28, p. 974–976.) **SPA**
Abstract of a paper read at the Congrès National d'Hygiène et de Salubrité Publique held at Marseilles, Oct. 7–13, 1906.

Venable, William Mayo. Garbage crematories in America. New York: J. Wiley & Sons, 1906. x, 200 p., 1 l. illus. 8°. **VDI**
Principles of design of every type of crematory built in the U. S. and a list of installations.

Weyl, Theodore. Über Müllentladestellen in Wohnquartieren. (Deutsche Vierteljahrschrift für öffentliche Gesundheitspflege. v. 38, p. 345–356. 4 illus.) **SPA**

Yarnall, D. Robert. Garbage disposal by reduction methods. ₁With discussion.₁ (Proc. Engineers' Club of Philadelphia. v. 23, p. 180–196.) **VDA**

—— Same, abstract. (Engineer, Chicago. v. 43, p. 732.) **VDA**

—— Same, abstract. (Municipal engineering. v. 31, p. 211–218.) **VDA**

1907

Abraham, A. J. Electricity and destructor works. 2000 w. (Electrical review. v. 60, p. 202.) †† **VGA**
Success of combined works for small towns and their failure for towns of 40,000 and upward.

Bordoni-Uffkeduzi, G. Les ordures de la rue et les ordures ménagères. (Giornale della R. Società Italiana d' Igiene. 1907, p. 97–117.) **SPA**

General Works, cont'd.

—— Same, condensed. (Annales d'hygiène publique. ser. 4, v. 9, p. 166-171.) **SPA**

Calder, William. Städtische Einrichtungen in den europäischen Ländern und den Vereinigten Staaten. (Zeitschrift für Transportwesen und Strassenbau. Jahrg. 24, p. 649-652.) **†† TPB**
A translation of article originally printed in the *Surveyor.* The original is not, at this time, in the Library.

Collection and disposal of city wastes. 2200 w. (Engineering record. v. 55, p. 635.) **†† VDA**
Review of a report by E. A. Fisher, city engineer Rochester, N. Y., commenting on disposal methods in different cities; recommending cremation.

Dettmar, G. Bedeutung der Müllverbrennung für die Elektrotechnik. 10,000 technische Zeitschrift. v. 28, p. 641-645, 670-672, 691-695, 712-716.) **†† VGA**

—— Same, condensed. (Journal für Gasbeleuchtung und Wasserversorgung. Jahrg. 51, p. 50-52.) **†† VOA**

—— Same, review. (L'Industrie electrique. v. 16, p. 493-494.) **†† VGA**
Types of furnaces in use in Brünn, Fiume, Hamburg and Zürich and the utilization of refuse for agricultural purposes or for electrical production.

Disposal of house refuse. (County and municipal record. v. 9, p. 210.) **SPA**

—— Same. (Engineering. v. 83, p. 753.) **†† VDA**
Description of the "lightning dust manipulator" for disintegrating, pulverizing and mixing refuse. Resulting mixture is available as a fertilizer.

Fetherston, J. T. Municipal refuse disposal. illus. 14,500 w., 1 diagr., 44 illus., 1 folding plate. (Proc. American Soc. Civil Engineers. p. 345.)

—— Same, condensed. (Engineering record. v. 56, p. 703.) **†† VDA**
Results of an investigation of local household refuse with a series of tests in burning mixed wastes. See also below, under 1908, Mitteilungen (Einige), etc.

Fried. Müllverbrennungsöfen. (Zeitschrift des Vereins Deutscher Ingenieure. Bd. 51, p. 305-306.) **VDA**

Guglielminetti. De l'hygiène des voies publiques. La lutte contre la poussière des routes. (Bericht über den 14. Internationalen Kongress für Hygiene und Demographie. v. 3, p. 332-347, illus.) **SPA**

—— Same, condensed. (Revue d'hygiène publique et de police sanitaire. v. 29, p. 933-934.) **SPA**

Horsfall Destructor Co., Ltd., Leeds. Catalogue. Review. (County and municipal Record. v. 8, p. 306.) **SPA**
A table showing date and place of erection of Horsfall destructors 1900 to 1902 is reproduced.

L'incinération des immondices par les destructeurs Heenan & Froude. (La technique sanitaire. Année 2, p. 63-64.) **SPA**

Lacomme, Léon. Incinération des ordures ménagères. (Revue pratique d'hygiène municipal. Année 3, p. 443-450.) **SPA**

Meyer, Karl M. Strassenreinigung im Winter. (Zeitschrift für Transportwesen und Strassenbau. Jahrg. 24, p. 266-270; illus.) **†† TPB**

Neuerungen auf dem Gebiete der Müllabfuhr. (Zeitschrift für Transportwesen und Strassenbau. Jahrg. 24, p. 240-243.) **†† TPB**
Dustproof transfer receptacles.

Perkins, Frank C. English, German and Swiss destructor plants. 2500 w. (Municipal engineering. v. 32, p. 371.) **VDA**

Potter, Alexander. Garbage disposal and street cleaning. (Municipal engineering. v. 33, p. 236-237.) **VDA**

Removal of ashes and garbage. 200 w. (Municipal journal and engineer. v. 23, p. 130.) **SERA**
Abstract of report to the Albany Medical Socy. giving statistics of methods and costs in 50 cities.

Schottelius, M. Ueber Strassenhygiene. (Bericht über den 14 Internationalen Kongress für Hygiene und Demographie. v. 3, p. 348-357.) **SPA**

Sprengwagen mit elektrischem Motorantrieb durch Strassenbahnen. (Zeitschrift für Transportwesen und Strassenbau. Jahrg. 24, p. 306-308; illus.) **†† TPB**
The motor sprinklers of Berlin, Cologne and Mannheim operated in connection with electric surface car system.

Thiessing, Hans. Beiträge zur Frage der Müllbeseitigung. (Archiv für Volkswohlfahrt. Jahrg. 1, p. 79-91; illus.) **† SA**

Thompson, W. Gilman. Street dirt and public health. (N. Y. Medical journal. v. 85, p. 723-726.) **WAA**

Ueber die Bedeutung der Müll- u. Canalisationsschlammverbrennung für die Elektrotechnik. 3000 w. (Elektrotechnische Rundschau. Dec. 24, 1907.) **†† VGA**
Garbage and sewage destructors from a hygienic point of view and their importance as sources of electric power.

1908

Beseitigung, Die, fester städtischer Abfallstoffe. (Zeitschrift für Transportwesen und Strassenbau. Jahrg. 25, p. 332-334.) **†† TPB**

Boulvois, H. Percy. On house refuse; collection and disposal. (Journal Sanitary Institute. v. 29, p. 176-179.) **SPA**

—— Road making in relation to street cleansing. (County and municipal record. v. 11, p. 289-290.) **SPA**
Read at the annual meeting in London of the Cleansing Superintendents.

—— Utilisation of residuals from refuse destructors. (Journal Sanitary Institute. v. 29, p. 624-630.) **SPA**

General Works, cont'd.

Coales, Herbert G. Coalesine fuel from refuse. (County and municipal record. v. 11, p. 142-143.)   **SPA**
Read at the Municipal Conference, London, May 7, 1908.

Final disposition of city refuse by mixed refuse destruction, and the final disposition of refuse in Great Britain. 1800 w., 3 diagr., 1 drawing. (Journal Society of Chemical Industry. v. 27, p. 380.)   **VOA**

Foster, E. H. Heenan refuse destructor. 400 w. (Journal of the Society of Chemical Industry. v. 27, p. 383.)   **VOA**

Garbage disposal data. 800 w. (Municipal journal and engineer. v. 25, p. 252.)   **SERA**
Notes on incinerators at Staten Island, Trenton, Allentown and reduction plants at Rochester and Syracuse.

Garbage reduction and incineration plants in the larger cities of the U. S. 2500 w. (Engineering news. v. 59, p. 284.)   †† **VDA**

Goodnough, X. H. The collection and disposal of municipal waste and refuse. (Assoc. Engineering Societies Journal. v. 11, p. 243-274.)   **VDA**

H. Verbrennungsversuche mit verschiedenen Müllarten im Dörrschen Müllverbrennungsofen. (Gesundheits-Ingenieur. Jahrg. 31, p. 664-667.)   †† **SPA**
Berlin, Stettin, Coblenz, Wiesbaden, Beuthen, Miskolez.

Hansen, Paul. City wastes disposal and street cleaning. 1500 w. (Engineering news. April 23, 1908.)   †† **VDA**
Abstract of a paper before the Ohio Engineering Socy.

Hering, Rudolph. Final disposal of refuse in American cities. 1000 w. (Journal of Society of Chemical Industry. v. 27, p. 380.)   **VOA**

Hilgermann. Lebensfähigkeit pathogener Keime in Kehricht und Müll. (Archiv für Hygiene. v. 65, p. 221-234.)   **SPA**

—— Same, reviewed. (Revue d'hygiène et de police sanitaire. v. 31, p. 598.) **SPA**

Kessler, Otto. Aesthetische und hygienische Förderungen der Strassenreinigung der Zukunft mit besonderer Berücksichtigung der Geldfrage. (Zeitschrift für Transportwesen und Strassenbau. Jahrg. 25, p. 3-5.)   †† **TPB**

Lévy, Georges. Utilisation des ordures ménagères. (La technique sanitaire. Année 3, p. 131-132.)   †† **SPA**

—— Same. (Annales d'hygiène publique. ser. 4, v. 10, p. 375-377.)   **SPA**

Mitteilungen, Einige, über englische Müllverbrennungsanlagen. (Zeitschrift für Transportwesen und Strassenbau. Jahrg. 25, p. 96-97.)   †† **TPB**
Based on the report of superintendent of street cleaning of the Borough of Richmond, N. Y. City, J. T. Fetherston; see above under 1907.

Nave, Félix. Considérations générales sur la destruction des immondices. (La technique sanitaire. Année 3, p. 274-286.)   †† **SPA**

—— Destruction des ordures ménagères. Comparaison entre l'incinération intégrale et la méthode mixte préconisée pour la fabrication des engrais organiques. (Revue d'hygiène et de police sanitaire. v. 30, p. 1105-1120.)   **SPA**

Parsons, Henry B. City refuse and its disposal. (California journal of technology. v. 12, no. 3, p. 28-36.)   **VA**

—— Same. (Journal Socy. of Chemical Industry. v. 27, p. 376-377.)   **VOA**

—— Same, with illus. (Scientific American suppl. v. 66, p. 8-12.)   †† **VA**

Refuse disposal in America. 1800 w. (Engineering record. v. 58, p. 85.)   †† **VDA**

Refuse disposal in Ohio. 800 w. (Municipal journal and engineer. v. 25, p. 776.)   **SERA**

Steele, W. J. Utilisation of residuals from refuse destructors. (Journal Sanitary Institute. v. 29, p. 631-637.)   **SPA**

—— Same, condensed. (County and municipal record. v. 11, p. 316-318.)   **SPA**

Thiessing, Hans. Neuere Erfahrungen auf dem Gebiete der Müllbeseitigung. (Gesundheits-Ingenieur. Jahrg. 31, p. 469-477.)   †† **SPA**

Utilisation comme engrais des gadoues et ordures ménagères. (Revue pratique d'hygiène municipale. Année 4, p. 161-164.)   **SPA**

Weiss, Eugène H. L'incinération des immondices dans les villes. 1674 w., 2 illus. (La nature. v. 70, p. 180.)   **OA**

—— Same. (Annales d'hygiène publique. ser. 4, v. 10, p. 74-77.)   **SPA**
Furnaces and methods in use in England and in Germany.

1909

Baskerville, Charles. City sanitation. (Report of the 10th annual conference of sanitary officers, State of New York. p. 127-131.)   **SPA**
Experimental plants a necessity in a growing city; methods of using street dirt; organization of a health department; the smoke problem.

Brandis. Die Wirtschaftlichkeit verschiedener Müllbeseitigungsverfahren. (Zeitschrift des Vereins Deutscher Ingenieure. Bd. 53, p. 1735-1740.)   **VDA**
Cleveland, Buffalo, Pforzheim, Hamburg, Wiesbaden and Frankfurt a. M. compared.

Brodie, John S. The collection and disposal of house refuse. (Journal Sanitary Institute. v. 31, p. 1-17.)   **SPA**

—— Same, condensed. (Surveyor and municipal and county engineer. Dec. 10, 1909, p. 676-677.)   †† **VDA**

General Works, cont'd.

Busch, August. Einiges über die Reinigung der Grossstädte. (Centralblatt für allgemeine Gesundheitspflege. v. 28, p. 337-345.) **SPA**

Dörr, Clemens. Die Müllanalyse und ihr praktischer Wert für die Müllverbrennung. (Zeitschrift für Stadthygiene. v. 1, p. 1-19.) **SPA**

Effenberger. Etwas über die Müllabfuhr. (Same. v. 1, p. 20-23.) **SPA**

Electricity from refuse. (Electrical engineer. April 16, 1909, p. 534-535.) **VGA**

Ende, Paul am. Review of work by Paul am Ende on air pollution by street dust. (Deutsche Vierteljahrsschrift für öffentliche Gesundheitspflege. v. 41, suppl. p. 594-596.) **SPA**

Fischer, J. C. H. Over vuilnisverbrandingsovens en daarmede te verkrijgen uitkomsten. (De Ingenieur. Jaarg. 24, p. 326-332.) **†† VDA**

Fours pour l'incinération des ordures ménagères. (Nouvelles annales de la construction. ser. 6, v. 6, col. 14-15; 89-96; 135-138; 157-158; 165-170; v. 7 col. 14-16; illus.) **†† VEA**
Port Ontario, Oak Park, Seattle, Newport Naval Training Station, Milwaukee furnaces described.

Goodnough, X. H. The collection and disposal of municipal refuse. h. t.-p. (Massachusetts. Health Board. 41. annual report, p. 405-423, 4 pl.) **SPB**

Greeley, Samuel A. Devices for charging refuse into high temperature refuse incinerators. 8000 w. (Engineering news. Aug. 26, 1909.) **†† VDA**

Hall, D. M. Incineration of city wastes with utilization. (American Public Health Assoc. Public health papers and reports. v. 35, pt. 1, p. 538-541; American journal of public hygiene. v. 20, p. 271-274.) **SPA**

Hering, Rudolph. Disposal of municipal refuse. (American journal of public hygiene. v. 19, p. 10-14.) **SPA**

Koeppen, Gustav. Die Beseitigung des Strassenstaubes. (Zeitschrift für Stadthygiene. v. 1, p. 244-253.) **SPA**

Loveday, William F. The design and working of a modern destructor. (County and municipal record. v. 13, p. 12-15.) **SPA**
Read at a metropolitan district meeting of the Incorporated Association of Municipal and County Engineers, London, March 26, 1909. Recent development and progress giving working results.

Mackay, George A. D. Some thought-currents of to-day and their bearing on the work of cleansing superintendents. (County and municipal record. v. 13, p. 220-223.) **SPA**
Read at the annual conference of cleansing superintendents, Glasgow, June 8-10, 1909.

Nave, Félix. Incinération des ordures ménagères. (L'Hygiène générale et appliquée. v. 4, p. 244.) **SPA**
Abstract of discussion at a session of the Société de médicine publique et de génie sanitaire, Feb. 24, 1909.

Parsons, Henry de B. City refuse and its diposal. (Engineering and contracting. September 1909, p. 186-189.) **VDA**

Robertson, J. A. Electricity works and refuse destructors. (County and municipal record. v. 13, p. 42-47, 61-63.) **SPA**

— Same. (Electrical engineer, London. v. 43, n. s., p. 42-47.) **VGA**
Benefits from combination of electricity works and refuse destructors.

Schottelius, M. Ueber Strassenstaub. (Zeitschrift für Stadthygiene. v. 1, p. 109-120.) **SPA**

Société de médicine publique et de génie sanitaire. Commission des ordures ménagères. Procès-verbaux des sessions 1-7. (Revue d'hygiène et de police sanitaire. v. 31, p. 696-702.) **SPA**

— Same. (Recommendations.) (L'Hygiène générale et appliquée. v. 4, p. 574-575.) **SPA**
The report was made in 1910; see below that date.

Soper, George A. Modern methods of street cleaning. London: A. Constable and Co., 1909. viii, 201 p., 25 pl. 8°. **VDH**

1910

Calder, William. Municipal waste. Its collection and disposal. (Surveyor and municipal and county engineer. January 7, 1910, p. 21-23; January 14, 1910, p. 51-52.) **†† VDA**
Australian methods.

Destruction, La, des gadoues par incinération dans les grandes villes. (Génie civil. v. 56, p. 395.) **†† VA**
Review of an article in L'Industria, Jan. 30, 1910. Study of cost of incineration; case of Frankfurt cited in particular.

English practice in the designing and working of a modern refuse destructor. (Chemical engineer. July 1910, p. 1-4.) **PKA**

Gordon, John. Notes on refuse destructors. (County and municipal record. v. 16, p. 223-224.) **SPA**
Relative fuel values of refuse and coal.

Hall, P. M. The Ten Commandments for Handling Garbage without Nuisance. (Report of the 10th annual conference of sanitary officers, State of New York, p. 119-126.) **SPA**
Elimination of the fly in garbage disposal; methods used in Minneapolis; progress of methods of garbage disposal; utilizing garbage for heating and lighting public buildings.

Hammond, E. K. The chemical utilization of municipal waste. (Chemical engineer. May 1910, p. 120-126.) **PKA**

General Works, cont'd.

Hering, Rudolph. Modern practice in garbage disposal. (Engineering record. v. 62, p. 361-363.)   †† **VDA**

Incinération des immondices. (La technique sanitaire. Année 5, p. 262-263.)   † **SPA**

Kern, Emile. Ordures ménagères. Conclusions du rapport présenté à la Société de médecine publique et de génie sanitaire au nom de la commission des ordures mènagères. (L'Hygiène générale et appliquée. v. 5, p. 289-290.)   **SPA**

Meyer, Friedrich. La technique de la combustion et l'utilisation de l'énergie des résidus des villes. (La technique sanitaire. Année 5, p. 309-316.)   † **SPA**

Morse, William F. The disposal of the city's waste. (The American city. v. 2, p. 119-122, 177-180, 223-227, 271-274.) **SERA**
Comparison of American cities.

—— High temperature garbage and refuse destructors. 3000 w. (Municipal engineering. Apr., 1910.)   **VDA**
Advantages of destructor over crematory system.

—— The practical questions in the collection and disposal of municipal waste. (Journal Assoc. of Engineering Societies. v. 45, p. 73-102, illus.)   **VDA**

Nave, Félix. L'utilisation, la transformation ou la destruction des ordures ménagères. (La technique sanitaire. Année 5, p. 252-259.)   † **SPA**

Refuse disposal in American cities. American attempts: resort to British practice: reduction. (Surveyor and municipal and county engineer. December 9, 1910. p. 782-783.)   †† **VDA**

Review, A, of practice in methods of refuse disposal in American cities, with figures of cost and efficiency, American crematory system. (Engineering and contracting. November 2, 1910, p. 384-388.)   **VDA**

Société de médecine publique et de génie sanitaire. Rapports et propositions de la commission nommée par la société pour l'étude de la question des ordures mènagères. (Revue d'hygiène et de police sanitaire. v. 32, p. 856-883, 1138-1146, 1266-1273. v. 33, p. 193-204.)   **SPA**
The commission was appointed on Feb. 24, 1909, and was composed as follows: Ach. Livache, president, Émile Kern, secretary, and Messrs. Ch. Dupuy, Loewy, Masson, Mazerolle, Nave, Tur and Vincey. The four reports of the commission are as follows: I. Collecte et enlèvement des ordures ménagères dans les maisons. Par M. Kern. II. Collecte sur la voie publique, évacuation et transport des ordures ménagères. Par M. Vincey. III. Utilisation, transformation ou destruction des ordures ménagères. Par M. Nave. IV. Utilisation agricole des ordures ménagères. Par M. Vincey.

Soper, George A. Modern methods of street cleaning. (Engineering news. v. 64, p. 97-98.)   †† **VDA**
Portions of an address before the New England Conference on street cleaning.

Specifications for determining cost of garbage incineration. (Engineering and contracting. August 24, 1910, p. 171-172.)   **VDA**

Street cleaning by vacuum process. (Municipal engineering. v. 38, p. 115.)   **VDA**

Watson, Hugh S. 1910. Cleansing departments in small burghs. (County and municipal record. v. 15, p. 212; 217.) **SPA**

—— Town scavenging and refuse disposal. (Municipal engineering. v. 38.)   **VDA**

[pt. 1.] Street cleaning. p. 1-3.
[pt. 2.] Special street cleaning services. p. 73-76.
[pt. 3.] Refuse collection and disposal. p. 143-144.
[pt. 4.] Disposal of house refuse. p. 229-234.
[pt. 5.] Types of destructors. p. 298-302.
Relates entirely to conditions in England.

Wilkinson, L. H. G. Some· profitable methods of utilising municipal waste. (Surveyor and municipal and county engineer. September 2, 1910, p. 327-328.)   †† **VDA**

1911

Blackham, Maj. R. J. The disposal of refuse in the tropics (i. e. India). (Journal Sanitary Institute. v. 32, p. 528-540.) **SPA**

Bredtschneider. Beseitigung und Verwertung des Hausmülls. (Gesundheits-Ingenieur. Jahrg. 34, p. 409-410.) †† **SPA**

Brown, Charles Carroll. Garbage and refuse collection and disposal. (Municipal engineering. v. 40, p. 106-114.)   **VDA**
Read before the Indiana Engineering Society.

Cost and efficiency of street cleaning methods. (Same. v. 40, p. 32-34.)   **VDA**
Chicago, Dayton, St. Louis, Albany, Cleveland, Scranton, Boston.

Davies, Francis H. The combustion of town refuse. 3000 w., illus. (Power, Aug. 1, 1911.)   †† **VDA**
Types of destructors and their operation.

Description of the matchless patented sanitary street cleaning machine. (Municipal engineering. v. 40, p. 376.)   **VDA**

Garbage collection and disposal. (Same. v. 40, p. 281-283.)   **VDA**
Table showing for last report year, either 1910 or 1911, the no. of wagons, horses, cans and the kind of disposal plant in operation in 121 American and two Canadian cities.

Greeley, Samuel A. Some observations upon the collection and disposal of garbage. 900 w. (Engineering news. Nov. 30, 1911.)   †† **VDA**
Outline of paper read before the N. J. Sanitary Assoc.

Hall, P. M. Garbage receptacles. (American Public Health Assoc. Journal. n. s. v. 1, p. 508-511.)   **SPA**

Hering, Rudolph. Modern practice in the disposal of refuse. (Same. n. s., v. 1, p. 910-919.)   **SPA**

General Works, cont'd.

Kewanee water-heating garbage burner. Catalogue no. 59. July, 1911. 20 p. illus. 8°.   **Room 115**

Landis, J. H.   Street dust and street cleaning in relation to health, comfort and economy. (Canadian engineer. June 8, 1911.)   **VDA**
Read before Boards of Health at Columbus, O.

Meyer, Friedrich.   La technique de la combustion et de la production d'énergie avec les résidus des villes. (La technique sanitaire. Année 6, p. 62-67, 85-88.) † **SPA**

Morse, William F.   Progress in city waste disposal during 1910. (The American city. v. 4, p. 32-36.)   **SERA**

Ohio. Health Board.   Report of a study of the collection and disposal of city wastes in Ohio. Supplement to the 25th annual report of the state board of health. 1911. 290 p. 8 pls. illus. 8°.   **VDI**

Regulations for collecting garbage at householders' expense. (Municipal engineering. v. 40, p. 348-350.)   **VDA**
Bay City, Mich., Duluth, Grand Rapids, Omaha, Salt Lake City.

Removing snow from roads and streets by spreading coal or earth upon the snow. (Engineering and contracting. January 25, 1911, p. 96.)   **VDA**

Watson, Hugh S.   Town scavenging and refuse disposal; a handbook of modern practice.   London: St. Bride's Press, Ltd., [1911]. 4 p.l., 75 (1) p., 2 plans. 8°. **VDI**

1912

Brook, John.   The proper disposal of domestic wastes in rural districts. 2000 w. (Surveyor. Jan. 19, 1912.)   †† **VDA**
Paper read before the Institute of Municipal Engineers at Birmingham, Eng.

Dörr, Clemens. Hausmüll und Strassenkehricht.   Leipzig, 1912. viii, 495 p., illus. 8°.   **VDH**

Greeley, Samuel A.   Methods of handling house refuse before collected by the city. 1800 w. (Engineering and contracting. May 15, 1912.)
Recommendations given before the N. J. Sanitary Assoc.

Knight, Ray R.   The destruction of house refuse by incineration. 4500 w. (Canadian engineer. Feb. 8, 1912.)   **VDA**

Lewis and KITCHEN. Catalogue no. 1-2. Refuse disposal.   Chicago, Ill. [1912.] ob. 8°.   †† **VDI**

Modern refuse disposal plants. 2500 w. (Municipal journal. May 30, 1912.)
Abstracts from the reports of Messrs. Hering and Gregory to the city of Toronto concerning the newest plants.

Skinner, J. J., and J. H. BEATTIE.   City street sweepings as a fertilizer. Washington, 1912. 8 p. 8°. (U. S. Soils Bureau. Circular 66.)

Story of the incinerite. [Catalogue.] Copyright by the National Incinerator Co., N. Y. 20 l. illus. 8°.   **Room 115**

Water heating by garbage burning. 2800 w. (Metal worker. June 21, 1912.) **VIA**

SPECIAL CITIES

Aachen, Germany.

1906

FUHRPARK und Strassenreinigung. (Bericht über die Verwaltung der Stadt Aachen, 1897/1906, p. 164-169.)   *****SYD**
In nature of a brief historical summary of each of the services of street cleaning and refuse removal.

1912

BEKANNTMACHUNG über die Strassenreinigung vom 17. April, 1912; [and] Polizeiverordnung betreffend Strassenreinigung vom 13. September, 1911. (Aachener Ortsrecht. Jahrg. 1912, p. 72-76.)   *****SYA**

Aberdeen.

1907

CLEANSING, The, of streets.   Important experiments at Aberdeen. (County and municipal record. v. 9, p. 223-224.)   **SPA**

1910

PROPOSED refuse destructor for Aberdeen. (County and municipal record. v. 14, p. 290.)   **SPA**
Abstract of report of the Cleansing Sub-committee to the town council.

Accrington, England.
See above under General Works, 1904.

Adelaide, South Australia.

1896

REPORT of the engineer and surveyor on garbage disposal for the city of Adelaide. n. t.-p. 4 p. 4°.   †† **SPI p.v.5, 22**

1900

SPECIFICATION for garbage destructor installation. n. t.-p. 21. 12°. and 1 l., 1 map. f°.   †† **VDI**

1907

SYNOPSIS of information re refuse destructors. 20 p. f°. (Notice, Papers, etc. of the council. 1906/7.)   *****SYB**
Summary of information relative to the destructors recently erected in the capitals of the Australian states, in the cities of New Zealand, and relative to destructors in use in Great Britain, obtained for the use of members of the council preparatory to erecting a destructor in Adelaide. Includes the report of the city surveyor of Prahran (W. Calder) on refuse destructors in Europe and elsewhere. 1907.

1908

SPECIFICATION for the supply and erection of refuse destructor installation for the city of Adelaide. 1908. 10, 9 p., 5 plates. f°. (Same. 1907/8.)   *****SYB**

Special Cities — Adelaide, cont'd.

1910

ADELAIDE's municipal enterprise. Rubbish destructor and allied works. Turning waste to profit. Adelaide, 1910. 3 l., illus. 4°. (Same. 1909/10.)   *SYB

Albany, N. Y.
See above under General Works, 1911.

Allegheny, Penn.
See above under General Works, 1894.

Allentown, Penn.
See above under General Works, 1908.

Altona, Germany.
STRASSENREINIGUNG und Abfuhrwesen. (Bericht über die Gemeinde-Verwaltung der Stadt Altona in den Jahren 1863 bis 1900. v. 3, p. 731-734.)   *SYD
Historical and tables of receipts and expenditures and operation from 1888/9 to 1899/1900.

Amsterdam, Netherlands.
See also above the General Works under dates of 1884 and 1899.
Verslag van den toestand der gemeente, 1877-1910.   *SYM
From 1877 to 1887 the hoofdstuk on Gemeente-eigendommen, Werken, etc. has a chapter on street cleaning only. Beginning with 1888 the street cleaning and refuse removal reports may be found as Reinigingsdienst under the hoofdstuk on Medische Politie.

Anderlecht, Belgium.
L'usine de démonstration d'incinération des immondices d'Anderlecht. Incinération a basse température. Système et procédé Tobiansky d'Althoff brevetés. (La technique sanitaire. Année 5, p. 320-321.)   †SPA

Atlanta, Ga.
New garbage furnace at Atlanta, Ga. 1,200 w. (In Engineering news. v. 45, p. 105.)   ††VDA

Atlantic City, N. J.

1894

SCULL, H. S. Garbage cremation in Atlantic City. (New Jersey. Board of Health. Annual report. 18, 1894, p. 29-32.)   SPB

1904

ATLANTIC City's garbage contract. (Municipal engineering. v. 27, p. 32.)   VDA
Synopsis of decision of Supreme Court of New Jersey setting aside the contract.

Ayr, Scotland.
NEW refuse destructor at Ayr. (County and municipal record. v. 5, p. 89-90.)
The municipal refuse disposal works with a Meldrum destructor were declared open on April 27, 1905.

Baltimore, Md.

Serial

Annual report of the Street Cleaning Department, 1882 (origin)-1909.   *SYA
Includes reports on garbage removal. In 1896 the Street Cleaning Department took over the work of collecting and removing dead animals heretofore done by the Health Board.

Non-serial
1901

AWARD of Baltimore garbage contract sustained. (Municipal engineering. v. 20, p. 240.)   VDA
Synopsis of decision of Circuit Court of Baltimore, March 8, 1901.

1903

GARBAGE, The, reduction plant at Baltimore. (Engineering record. v. 47, p. 633.)   ††VDA
WILLEY, Day Allan. Baltimore's system of garbage disposal. 700 w., 4 illus. (Scientific American. v. 89, p. 308.)   ††VA

1906

STREET cleaning in Baltimore. (Municipal engineering. v. 30, p. 292.)   VDA

Barmen, Germany.
STRASSENREINIGUNG einschliesslich Beseitigung von Schnee und Eis, Müllabfuhr und Müllverbrennung, 1901-1910. (Bericht über die Verwaltung und den Stand der Gemeinde-Angelegenheiten, 1901-1910.)   *SYD
The report on street cleaning appears for the first time in 1901 and annually thereafter, snow and ice removal appear annually beginning with 1907, refuse removal beginning 1905 and refuse incineration beginning 1907.

Bath, England.

1896

BATH refuse destructors. 1300 w. 21 drawings. (Engineering. v. 61, p. 12.)   VDA

Bay City, Mich.
See also above, General Works, under date of 1911.

1906

TEXT of ordinance of Bay City, Mich. relative to the removal of garbage. (Municipal engineering. v. 40, p. 349.)   VDA
—— Same. (In: Bay City. Charter and ordinances. 1907, p. 256-258.)   *SYA

Bellshill, Scotland.

1908

DOBSON, James. The advantages of a daily system of collection of refuse. (County and municipal record. v. 11, p. 140-141.)
Relates to Bellshill, county of Lanark; population 14,134.

Berlin, Germany.
See also above the General Works, under the dates of 1884, 1896, 1898, 1899, 1907 and 1908 resp.

Serial

BERICHT über die Gemeinde-Verwaltung der Stadt Berlin. 1861/76-1901/5.   *SYD
Each issue contains a chapter: "Reinigung und Besprengung der Strassen; Müllbeseitigung," as follows: 1861/76, v. 2, p. 81-91; 1877/81, v. 2, p. 59-65. 1882/88, v. 2, p. 36-43; 1889/95, v. 1, p. 102-112; 1895/1900, v. 1, p. 164-172; 1901/5, v. 1, p. 122-130. The material in the issue for 1861/71 comprises an historical résumé of the street cleaning methods of Berlin from 1660. There is also a table of receipts and expenditures and of operation for 1861-1875.
BERICHT über die Verwaltung der Feuerwehr, Telegraphie, polizeilichen und städ-

Special Cities — Berlin, cont'd.

tischen Strassenreinigung, 1871-1874. (Verwaltungsbericht des Magistrats, 1871-1874.)   **＊SYD**

Continued as:

BERICHT über das städtische Strassenreinigungswesen, 1875, 1888/9, 1896/7-1910. (Verwaltungsbericht des Magistrats, 1875, 1888/9, 1896/7-1910.)   **＊SYD**
Beginning with 1888/9 the reports include material on snow and ice removal and refuse removal. Each report up to 1901 includes cumulative tables of receipts, expenditures and operation from 1876. The 1896/7 report has an especial report on the transport feature of refuse removal, which is reprinted in Zeitschrift für Transportwesen, etc. v. 15, p. 86.

MONATSBERICHTE des statistischen Amts der Stadt Berlin, 1903-1912.   **†† SDN**
1903-1909 incomplete. Contains current street cleaning and refuse and snow removal statistics.

Non-serial

1893

NEUE, Die, Berliner Polizei-Verordnung betr. die Müllabladeplätze. (Zeitschrift für Transportwesen und Strassenbau. v. 10, p. 334-335.)   **TPB**

1895

ANLAGE zur Verarbeitung städtischer Abfallstoffe. (Zeitschrift für Transportwesen und Strassenbau. v. 12, p. 4-6, 18-20; illus.)   **TPB**

MÜLLVERBRENNUNGSVERSUCHE, Die, der Stadt Berlin. (Revue d'hygiène et de police sanitaire. v. 17, p. 1133-1134.)   **SPA**
—— Same. (Minutes of Proc. Institute of Civil Engineers. v. 122, p. 443-444.)   **VDA**
Both of these articles are reviews of an article which appeared originally in the Gesundheits-Ingenieur of July 15, 1895. The original is, at this time, not in the Library.

POLIZEI-VERORDNUNG. ıText of §100 relating to refuse removal. Jan. 30, 1895.ı (Zeitschrift für Transportwesen und Strassenbau. v. 12, p. 99-101.)   **TPB**

STÄDTISCHE, Die, Müllverbrennungs-Anlage vor dem Stralauer Thor in Berlin. (Annalen für Gewerbe und Bauwesen. Bd. 37, p. 209-21.)   **VDA**
—— Same, reviewed. (Minutes of Proc. Institute of Civil Engineers. v. 124, p. 469-470.)   **VDA**

1896

INDUSTRIELLE, Die, Verwerthung des Berliner Hausmülls. (Zeitschrift für Transportwesen und Strassenbau. v. 13, p. 287.)   **TPB**

MÜLLBESEITIGUNGSFRAGE, Die, in Berlin. (Same. v. 13, p. 72-74, 105, 178.)   **TPB**

MÜLLVERBRENNUNGS-VERSUCHE, Die, der Stadt Berlin. (Same. v. 13, p. 183-184.)   **TPB**

THIESS, F. Die Strassenreinigung der Stadt Berlin mit besonderer Berücksichtigung der Reinigung von Asphaltstrassen. (Same. v. 13, p. 447-449, 463-464.)   **TPB**

1897

AHNHUDT, N. Die Berliner Müllabfuhr und die Müllbeseitigung durch Schmelzen

des Mülles. (Zeitschrift für Transportwesen und Strassenbau. v. 14, p. 132-133.)   **TPB**

BOHM, and Grohn. Die Müllverbrennungsversuche in Berlin. (Same. v. 14, p. 500-502, 521-522.)   **TPB**
—— Same, reviewed. (Centralblatt für allgemeine Gesundheitspflege. v. 17, p. 106-107.)   **SPA**
—— Same, reviewed. (Minutes of Proc. Institute of Civil Engineers. v. 131, p. 413-414.)   **VDA**

HERING, Rudolph. Disposal of garbage and refuse; cost of construction and operation of the Berlin, Ger., works. 9,500 w., 14 drawings. (Engineering record. v. 36, p. 532, 558.)
Experiments with Horsefall and Warren furnaces indicate that English system is not applicable to Berlin. Coal must be added to aid combustion unless refuse has been sifted. Dry-air blast seems necessary also.

MÜLLABFUHR, Die, Berlins. (Zeitschrift für Transportwesen und Strassenbau. v. 14, p. 61-62, 79, 109-110, 127, 282, 495.)   **TPB**

RÖHRECKE, B. Müllabfuhr in Berlin. (Same. v. 14, p. 14-15.)   **TPB**
Brief synopsis of an address before the Berliner Grundbesitzer-Verein.

WEYL, Theodore. Ein Gutachten über die Müllbeseitigung ıvon Berlinı. (Same. v. 14, p. 17-19.)   **TPB**
Statement made at the request of the Wirthschaftsgenossenschaft Berliner Grundbesitzer.

ZUR Frage der Müllbeseitigung ıin Berlinı. (Same. v. 14, p. 4-5.)   **TPB**

1898

EGER, P. ıDie Müllbeseitigung in Berlin.ı (Zeitschrift für Transportwesen und Strassenbau. v. 15, p. 286-287.)   **TPB**
Synopsis of discussion of a paper read at a session of the Deutsche Gesellschaft für öffentliche Gesundheitspflege.

MÜLLABFUHR für Berlin. (Same. v. 15, p. 198-200, 214, 310, 327, 389.)   **TPB**

1899

EGER, P. Die Beseitigung des Hausmülls. (Gesundheits-Ingenieur. Jahrg. 22, p. 56-57.)   **†† SPA**
Refers to the dustproof Kinsbruner removal system in use in Berlin.

HAENTZSCHEL, W. Der neue Müllschmelzofen in Berlin, System "Wegener." (Gesundheits-Ingenieur. v. 22, p. 172-173.)   **†† SPA**

MÜLLSCHMELZVERFAHREN in Berlin. (Zeitschrift für Transportwesen und Strassenbau. v. 16, p. 160, 227, 258, 370, 546.)   **TPB**

ZUR Anlegung eines neuen grossen Abladeplatzes in Berlin. (Same. v. 16, p. 482.)   **TPB**

1900

BERLINER, Das, Srassenreinigungswesen. (Zeitschrift für Transportwesen und Strassenbau. v. 17, p. 424-426.)   **TPB**

EıGERı, P. Zur Frage der Beseitigung des Berliner Hausmülls. (Gesundheits-Ingenieur. Jahrg. 23, p. 242-244.)   **†† SPA**

HıAENTZSCHELı, W. Zur Frage der Beseitigung des Berliner Hausmülls. (Same. Jahrg. 23, p. 140-141.)   **†† SPA**

Special Cities — Berlin, cont'd.

—— Same, reviewed. (Minutes of Proc. Inst. Civil Engineers. v. 142, 437.)   **VDA**

STRASSENREINIGUNG von Berlin. (Zeitschrift für Transportwesen und Strassenbau. v. 17, p. 563.)   **TPB**
Synopsis of a conference held in the Prussian Police Department relative to the care of the streets in rain and fog to prevent accidents to man and animals.

ZUR Müllfrage in Berlin. (Same. v. 17, p. 258, 276, 308, 388.)   **TPB**

1901

RÖHRECKE, B. Berlins Müllabfuhr 1901. (Fortschritte der Strassenhygiene. Heft 1, p. 32-43, 6 illus.)   **†VDH**

1902

ZUR Frage der Müllabfuhr (in Berlin). (Zeitschrift für Transportwesen und Strassenbau. v. 19, p. 17, 347, 395, 408.)   **TPB**

1903

HYGIENISCHE Müllverwerthung System Bauer (in Berlin). (Zeitschrift für Transportwesen und Strassenbau. Jahrg. 22, p. 463-466.)   **††TPB**

1905

HENTIG. Die Verwertung des Berliner Mülls. (Zeitschrift für Transportwesen und Strassenbau. Jahrg. 22, p. 18-20.)   **††TPB**

ZUR Frage der Müllbeseitigung in Berlin. (Same. Jahrg. 22, p. 298-299.)   **††TPB**

1906

BERLINER Gemeinderecht. Bd. 9. Strassenreinigung, etc. 398 p. 8°.   ***SYD**

1907

MÜLLABFUHRWAGEN mit einem zur Aufnahme des Müllkastens bestimmten, an Schienen geführten hochziehbaren Schlitten. (Zeitschrift für Transportwesen und Strassenbau. Jahrg. 24, p. 445-446; illus.)   **††TPB**
The Kinsbruner apparatus used in Berlin.

1908

STREET, A, cleaning automobile (in Berlin, Germany). (Municipal engineering. v. 34, p. 266-267; 1 illus.)   **VDA**

1909

CONNER, Edward. Street cleaning in Berlin. (County and municipal record. v. 13, p. 505-506.)   **SPA**

1910

DÖRR, Clemens, editor. Denkschrift betreffend Errichtung einer Versuchsanstalt für Beseitigung und Verwertung von Hausmüll und Strassenkehricht in Berlin. Ueberreicht von der städtischen Müllverwertungs- u. Versuchsanstalt, Berlin. (Archiv für Stadthygiene. Jahrg. 1910, Heft 3.)
The original is not, at this time, in the Library.

—— Same, abstracted. (Gesundheits-Ingenieur. Jahrg. 33, p. 791.)   **††SPA**

1911

BERLIN waste utilization plant. 1000 w. (Municipal journal and engineer. v. 30, p. 291.)   **††SER**

HERING, Rudolph. Data on street-cleaning efficiency in Berlin. 5000 w. (Engineering news. May 18, 1911.)   **††VDA**

1912

BERLIN's model sanitation. Its modern system of sewage and garbage disposal. 350 w. newspaper clipping.   **Room 229**

Bermondsey, England.

1902

BERMONDSEY. Electric lighting and dust destructor works. Souvenir. January 23, 1902. n. p., n. d. 30 p., 5 plans, 16 plates. 12°.   **VGS**

BERMONDSEY combined refuse destructor and electricity supply works. 4,800 w., 17 drawings, 5 illus. (Electrical engineer. o. s. v. 35 (n. s. v. 29), p. 117, 153-156.)   **††VGA**
Claimed that the institution constitutes a part of the most complete and up-to-date municipal undertaking to be found in the United Kingdom.

Beuthen, Germany.
See above General Works under date of 1908.

Birkenhead, England.

1874

REPORT of the medical officer of health on the removal and disposal of town refuse with commentary. Birkenhead (1874). 16 p. 8°.   **VDI p.box 1**

Birmingham, England.
See also above, the General Works, under dates of 1888 and 1898.

ANNUAL report of the city engineer and surveyor, 1899-1909/10.   **VDDA**
Includes report on street cleansing, watering and refuse removal. Each report includes a triennial cumulative table showing quantity of sweepings, etc. removed.

Blackburn, England.
See also above, General Works, under dates of 1901 and 1904.

ANNUAL report of the medical officer of health, 1902-1911.   **SPC**
From 1902-1904 there is only a tabular statement of the operation of the destructors; in 1905 there is a brief description of each destructor, and the reports thereafter include a statistical return of the operations of each of the four destructors.

Blackpool, England.
See also above, the General Works, under date of 1888.

1909

BRODIE. John S. The collection and disposal of house refuse. (Journal of the Sanitary Institute. v. 31, p. 1-17.)   **SPA**

—— Same. (County and municipal record. v. 14, p. 257-259.)   **SPA**
The Journal of the Sanitary Institute prints the discussion on the article; this is not included in the County and municipal record. The subject matter relates largely to Blackpool.

Bloomington, Ill.

1911

TEXT of ordinance regulating disposal of refuse; August 5. (U. S. Public Health and Marine Hospital Service. Public health reports. v. 27, p. 196.)   **SPB**

Special Cities, cont'd.

Bochum, Germany.

1901

ASSMANN, W. Strassenhygiene in Bochum. (Fortschritte der Strassenhygiene. Heft 1, p. 1-32, 6 illus.)   †VDH

Bolton, England.
See above General Works, under date of 1888.

Bombay, India.

1885

Refuse-destructor at Bombay. 600 w., 5 drawings. (Sanitary engineer. v. 13, p. 108.)   ††VDA

Bordeaux, France.
See above, General Works, under date of 1884.

Boston, Mass.
See also above, General Works, under date of 1911.

1854

COMPLAINT of citizens and hotel keepers to the mayor and aldermen against present system of removal of offal. 7 p. 8°. (City doc. 73, 1854.)   •SYA

1879

CLARKE, Eliot C. City scavenging at Boston. Read at the seventh annual meeting of the American Public Health Association. Nashville, Tenn., Nov. 18, 1879. n. p. [1879?] 8 p. 8°.   VDI p.box 4
—— Same. (American Public Health Assoc. Public health reports and papers. v. 5, p. 24-31.)
Mr. Clarke was principal asst. engineer in charge of improved sewerage, Boston.

1895

ARNOLD system of garbage utilization at Boston. 2,500 w., 4 drawings, 6 illus. (Engineering news. v. 33, p. 211.)   ††VDA
Garbage is subjected to action of steam and the vapors are condensed. Grease, tankage and water are separated and the tankage is pressed and dried, then to be used as fertilizer.

1899

UTILIZATION of city refuse in Boston, Mass. 1800 w., 4 illus. (Engineering record. v. 39, p. 277.)   ††VDA

1901

HILL, Hibbert Winslow. Refuse disposal in Boston. (American Public Health Assoc. Public health papers and reports. v. 27, p. 186-193.)   SPA
With a map showing refuse disposal in Boston. Preceded by a historical summary of methods.
GARBAGE reduction plant at Boston, Mass. 3,000 w., 2 drawings, 2 illus. (Engineering record. v. 44, p. 251.)   ††VDA
Arnold reduction process combined with a method of ammonia recovery, with use of by-product coke-ovens.
See also editorial, p. 241.
MORSE, W. F. Utilizing Boston's refuse. (Municipal journal and engineer. v. 10, p. 117-119.)   ††SER

1902

GARBAGE disposal problem in Boston and elsewhere. 2,000 w. (In Engineering news. v. 48, p. 96.)   ††VDA
Editorial discussion of operation of reduction works in Boston.

1908

GOODNOUGH, X. N. The collection and disposal of municipal waste and refuse. 9000 w. (Journal Assoc. of Engineering Societies. v. 40, p. 423.)   VDA
Refers particularly to refuse of Boston.
REPORT of the special commission to investigate questions affecting the collection and disposition of garbage and offal in the city of Boston. Submitted Nov. 8, 1908. Boston, 1908. 25 p. 8°.   VDIA

1909

GARBAGE collection. (The American city. v. 1, p. 105-106.)   SERA
Boston.
STUDY, A, of street cleaning conditions in Boston, with data on the cost of snow removal, push-cart patrol system, machine sweeping and maintenance of horses. 5500 w. (Engineering and contracting. Dec. 22, 1909.)   †VDA

1910

ODOURLESS, An, garbage wagon. (The Surveyor and municipal and county engineer. February 18, 1910, p. 253.)   ††VDA
REPORT of the second special commission appointed to investigate the subject of the collection and disposal of refuse in the city. Submitted Jan. 31, 1910. Boston, 1910. 32 p., 1 diagr. 8°.   VDIA
—— Same, reviewed. (Municipal engineering. v. 38, p. 209.)   VDA
—— Same, reviewed. 4500 w. (Engineering news. Feb. 10, 1910.)   ††VDA

1911

COST of bids for disposal of refuse. [Proceedings in City Council.] (Boston. City record. v. 3, p. 953-954.)   •SYA
DISPOSAL of refuse. Reports of special commissions submitted to the mayor Nov. 8, 1908, and Jan. 31, 1910, and proposals received by the commissioner of public works April 24, 1911. n. t.-p. 94 p. 8°. (Document 82-1911.)
FINANCE Commission. [Report on the refuse refusal contract.] (Boston. City record. v. 3, p. 983-985.)   •SYA
SPECIFICATIONS for a 10-year refuse disposal contract, Boston, Mass. 2500 w. (Engineering news. Nov. 23, 1911.)   ††VDA

1912

GARBAGE box plan fails. 460 w. newspaper clipping.   Room 229
GARBAGE disposal contract. [Text of contract and of specifications.] (Boston. City record. v. 4, p. 109-115.)   •SYA
REPORT of a committee of the Chamber of Commerce of Boston on disposal of refuse. (Boston. City record. v. 4, p. 41-42.)   •SYA

Bradford, England.
See also above General Works, under date of 1899.

Serial

Annual report of the medical officer of health, 1880-1881, 1900-1904, 1906.   SPC
Contains an annual report on the collection and disposal of refuse.

Special Cities — Bradford, cont'd.

Non-serial

1900

DISPOSAL of refuse in Bradford. 4000 w., 1 drawing. (Engineering. v. 70, p. 383.)
†† VDA
—— Same. (Electrical review, London. v. 47, p. 415-418.)   †† VGA
—— Same, abstract. 500 w. (Engineering record. v. 42, p. 297.)   †† VDA
—— Same, condensed. (Minutes of Proc. Institution of Civil Engineers. v. 144, p. 407-409.)   VDA
Reviews operation of plant during 20 years and describes a test of 12 cells during 278 hours.

1904

CALL, Ernest. City of Bradford destructors. (County and municipal record. v. 3, p. 247-249.)   SPA

1906

FORBÁT, Emerich. Abwasserreinigung und Kehrichtbeseitigung der Stadt Bradford in England. (Gesundheits-Ingenieur. Jahrg. 29, p. 121-127.)   SPA
—— Same, reviewed. (Hygienisches Zentralblatt. v. 1, p. 198-199.)   SPA

1908

HORSEFALL destructor. 2,500 w., 6 drawings. (Engineering. v. 66, p. 200.) †† VDA
Plant at Bradford, Eng. is described.

Braunschweig, Germany.
See also above, General Works, under the date of 1898.

1758

Serenissimi gnädigste Verordnung die Strassenreinigung in der Stadt Braunschweig betreffend. Braunschweig, 1758. 8 p. 16°.

Bremen, Germany.
See also above, General Works, under the date of 1898.

Serial

BERICHT der Strassenreinigungsverwaltung.
The Library has, at this time, no separate copies. The reports for 1905/6–1907/8 are printed in Zeitschrift für Transportwesen und Strassenbau.
†† TPB, v. 23–25, resp.

Non-serial

1902

GÜNTHER. Neuorganisation der Strassenreinigung und Müllabfuhr in Bremen. (Zeitschrift für Transportwesen und Strassenbau. v. 19, p. 317-320.)   TPB
STRASSENREINIGUNG und Müllabfuhr. Bericht der Senats Deputation für Strassenreinigung. (Verhandlungen zwischen Senat und Bürgerschaft. 1902, p. 411-423.)   *SYD

1903

TJADEN. Die Strassenreinigung und die Müllabfuhr (in Bremen). (Zeitschrift für Transportwesen und Strassenbau. rg. 22, p. 519.)   †† TPB

1907

BERICHT der (Senat) Deputation für die Strassenreinigung über den Ankauf von Grundstücken zur Ablagerung von Hausmüll. (Verhandlungen zwischen Senat und Bürgerschaft. 1907, p. 152-155, 174-175, 211, 213.)   *SYD
GRAEPEL, R. Strassenreinigung und Abfuhr des Hausunrates. (In: Tjaden. Bremen in hygienischer Beziehung. p. 132-138.)   SPL

1908

BERICHT der (Senat) Deputation für Strassenreinigung über den Ankauf von Grundstücken zur Ablagerung von Hausmüll. (Verhandlungen zwischen Senat und Bürgerschaft. 1908, p. 1221-1225.)   *SYD
NEUORGANISATION der Strassenreinigung. (Verhandlungen zwischen Senat und Bürgerschaft. 1908, p. 695-696.)   *SYD

Breslau, Germany.
VERWALTUNGSBERICHT des Magistrats, 1889-/92-1907/10.   *SYD
Under the heading of Marstall und Strassenreinigung there is an annual report on the street cleaning and scavenging services.

Bridgeport, Conn.

1898

CHARTER and ordinances. Revised edition. Bridgeport, 1898. 302 p. 8°. *SYA
Chap. 21, sec. 173–183 (p. 149–150) comprise the garbage removal ordinance.

Brighton, England.

1906

WELLER, Alfred. Usine pour la destruction des ordures ménagères à Brighton (Sussex, Angleterre). (L'Hygiène générale et appliquée. v. 1, p. 731.)   SPA

Bristol, England.

1904

HARDING, H. W. Refuse destructor installations. (County and municipal record. v. 4, p. 198-199.)   SPA
On various types of destructors. Paper read at a meeting of the Bristol Association of Engineers.

Bromberg, Germany.
VERWALTUNGS-BERICHT des Magistrats, 1883/8-1892/3, 1894/5, 1896/7-1897/8. *SYD
Under the heading Strassenreinigungs- und Abfuhr Anstalt there is an annual report on street cleaning and refuse removal.

Brookline, Mass.   1911

TEXT of ordinance regulating disposal of refuse; Nov. 6. (U. S. Public Health and Marine Hospital Service. Public health reports. v. 27, p. 266.)   SPB

Brooklyn, N. Y.

1896

LOCKE, William W. Report on plumbing work and garbage disposal. (Brooklyn, N. Y. Health Department. Annual report for the 11 months ending Nov. 30, 1896, p. 601-608.)   *SYA
This is the edition of the Health Department report bound up in the collected documents of Brooklyn.
LOCKE, William W., and J. B. TAYLOR. Reports on I. Garbage disposal in the outlying wards. II. History of the garbage

Special Cities — Brooklyn, cont'd.

contract. III. Refuse disposal of cities.
1896. 120 p. 8°.   **VDI p.v.12, 7**
—— Same. (Brooklyn, N. Y. Health
Department. Annual report for the 12
months ended Dec. 31, 1896, p. 227-364.)
                                    SPB p.box
There are two annual reports for 1896, viz. one
dated Jan. 1, 1897 covers preceding 12 months, and
one dated Dec. 14. 1896, covers the preceding 11
months.

1906

KEHRICHT- und Müllbeseitigung in Brooklyn. (Zeitschrift für Transportwesen und
Strassenbau. Jahrg. 23, p. 601-604; illus.)
                                    †† TPB
RUBBISH incinerator plant in Brooklyn.
3,000 w., 4 drawings, 3 illus. (Engineering
record. v. 54, p. 214.)   **†† VDA**
Incineration of light refuse supplies steam for a
railway repair shop and for a brewery.

Brünn, Austria.
See also above General Works, under the date of
1907.

1906

KANDER, Sigmund. Müllverbrennungs-
Anlage der Stadtgemeinde Brünn. 5,000
w., 1 diagr., 5 drawings, 5 illus. (Elektrotechnik und Maschinenbau. v. 24, p. 721,
741.)   **†† VGA**
Information on the Custodis refuse destructor
and the steam plant at Brünn, Austria.

1907

USINE d'incinération des gadoues de la
ville de Brünn. 1,600 w., 5 drawings. (Le
génie civil, v. 50, p. 199.)   **†† VA**
Description of incinerating plant at Brünn, Austria, with utilization of heat.

Brussels, Belgium.
See also above General Works under dates of
1884, 1894 and 1899 resp.

Serial

SERVICE du nettoyage et de la voirie.
[Rapport annuel,] 1902-1910. (In: Rapport
fait au conseil communale par le collège
des bourgmestre et echevins.)   **∗ SYN**
Includes street cleaning and refuse removal, and,
from 1903, refuse incineration. The incinerator was
put into operation on July 24, 1903. The estimated
cost of construction is given on p. 211 of the report
for 1901 and on p. 269 of the report for 1902. The
report for 1910 contains, p. 581 et seq., a special
report by Dr. Van Campenhout, connected with the
plant, on the operation of the Brussels incinerator,
apropos of the Brussels Exposition of 1910.

Non-Serial
1895

STRASSENREINIGUNG, Die, in Brüssel. (Zeitschrift für Transportwesen und Strassenbau. v. 12, p. 516-518.)   **†† TPB**
1898

STADELMANN, A. Studien-Reise des Stras-
seninspectors der Stadt Zürich vom Juli
1898. (Zeitschrift für Transportwesen und
Strassenbau. v. 16, p. 80-84, 292-296, 308-
311, 325-326, 454-457, 471-472, 486-489, 502-
504, 518-521, 535-536; illus.)   **†† TPB**
Report of a tour of inspection in the cities of
Frankfurt a. M., Cologne, Brussels, London and
Paris. While the report relates primarily to street
building, there is a good deal of material on street
cleaning.

1903

LEWIS, J. La nouvelle usine d'incinération des immondices de la ville de Bruxelles. (Annales des travaux publiques de
Belgique. ser. 2, v. 8, p. 647-675.) **VDDA**
STABILIMENTO, Lo, per l'incenerimento
delle immondezze di Bruxelles. 1 pl.
(Giornale del genio civile. Anno 41, p. 291-
297.)   **VDA**
1904

NEW refuse destructors at Brussels.
(Sanitary record. v. 33, p. 2.)   **† SPA**
WATSON, George. Burning of town refuse, with special reference to the destructors at Brussels, West Hartlepool, Moss
Side and Westminster. 9,000 w., 1 diagr.,
10 drawings, 4 illus. Discussion, 2,000 w.
(Transactions American Soc. of Mechanical Engineers. v. 25, p. 1074.)   **VFA**
1905

L'USINE d'incinération des immondices
de la ville de Bruxelles. (Revue univer-
selle des mines. sér. 4, v. 11, p. 267-289.)
                                    VA

Budapest, Hungary.
1896

KEHRICHT-ABFUHR mittels Eisenbahn.
(Zeitschrift für Transportwesen und Strassenbau. v. 13, p. 464.)   **†† TPB**
Description of the special refuse removal railway
constructed by L. v. Cséry.
ELEKTRISCHE Verwertung des Stadtmülls
von Budapest. (Elektrotechnische Zeitschrift. Jahrg. 17, p. 652.)   **†† VGA**
—— Same. (Zeitschrift für Transportwesen und Strassenbau. Jahrg. 13, p. 582.)
                                    †† TPB
1897

MÜLL-ABFUHR, Die, in Budapest. (Zeitschrift für Transportwesen und Strassenbau. v. 14, p. 333-335.)   **†† TPB**
Advance report of representatives of the Magis-
trate of Berlin and of the Prussian Police Department of an inspection of the Budapest method of
dustless refuse removal.

1908

BALLÓ, Alfred. Das Reinigungswesen
der Haupt- und Residenzstadt Budapest.
(Zeitschrift für Transportwesen und Strassenbau. Jahrg. 25, p. 673-674, 693-694, 720-
721, 738-739, 759-760; illus.)   **†† TPB**
1911

BALLÓ, Alfred. Das Reinigungswesen
der Haupt- und Residenzstadt Budapest.
15 p. 8°.
KÖZLEKEDÉSI, A, ügyosztály elöterjeszté-
se a szemételtávolitás kérdésének rende-
zése tárgyában. 36 p. f°.
Report in regard to waste removal.

Buenos Aires, Argentine Republic.
Serial

ANNUARIO estadistico, 1891-1908. **SDG**
Each year contains a report on public cleansing.
The Annuario is issued in a French, English and a
Spanish edition. The Library has some of each.
In the Spanish edition see the division under Lim-
pieza pubblica, in the French under Nettoyage pu-
blique.

Special Cities — Buenos Aires, cont'd.

MONTHLY bulletin of municipal statistics, 1888-1912.   †† SDG
Each month a report is made on the public cleaning service as follows: Number of trips, household refuse, incineration, street sweepings, sweeping machine, sweeping by hand, atmospherical refuse carts (sic), dead animals, water-cart service, and municipal inspection.

Non-Serial
1905

AUF dem Strassenbahngleis laufender Sprengwagen für Buenos-Ayres. (Zeitschrift für Transportwesen und Strassenbau. Jahrg. 22, p. 412.)   †† TPB

Buffalo, N. Y.
See also above General Works under dates of 1894 and 1909.

Serial

ANNUAL report of the bureau of streets, 1-17. 1893-1909/10. (In: Buffalo. Public Works Department. Annual report, 1893-1909/10.)   VDDA
The superintendent of streets in his first report says: "The principal divisions of the bureau may be considered under the heads of street cleaning, ash and garbage collection and disposition, public lighting, cleaning of sewers, while the minor divisions are sprinkling, builders' permits, street signs, etc.
ANNUAL report of the refuse utilization plant, 1-2. 1908/9-1909/10. (In: Buffalo. Public Works Department. Annual report, 17-18. 1908/9-1909/10.)   VDDA

Non-serial
1898

STREET cleaning in Buffalo. (Municipal engineering. v. 15, p. 309.)   VDA

1899

REPORT from the commissioner of public works showing moneys expended for the collection and removal of ashes and garbage from 1893 to 1899. (Proc. Common Council. 1899, p. 980-984.)   * SYA
Preceded by specifications for removal from 1899 to 1903.

1901

COMMUNICATIONS from the commissioner of public works relative to garbage contracts. (Proc. Common Council. 1901, p. 1419-1420, 2104-2107.)   * SYA

1902

COMMUNICATION from the commissioner of public works urging measures to at once improve the service in the collection of garbage and ashes. (Proc. of the Common Council. 1902, p. 1160-1161.)   * SYA
COMMUNICATION from commissioner of public works relative to collection of ashes and garbage. (Same. 1902, p. 1586-1587.)   * SYA
COMMUNICATION from the commissioner of public works with recommendations looking to improvement in the collection of ashes and garbage. (Same. 1902, p. 1160-1161.)   * SYA
LANDRETH, Olin H. The disposal of refuse in the city of Buffalo, N. Y. (American Public Health Assoc. Public health reports and papers. v. 28, p. 51-58.)   SPA

REPORT of committee on sanitary matters relative to collection of ashes and garbage. (Proc. Common Council. 1902, p. 1586-1587.)   * SYA
TEXT of Mayor's veto message relative to resolution authorizing the commissioner of public works to make a contract for garbage removal. (Proc. Common Council. 1902, p. 898-899.)   * SYA

1903

SOME features of the new garbage reduction works at Buffalo, N. Y. 700 w. (Engineering news. v. 49, p. 202.) †† VDA
Includes abstract of paper by C. A. Blessing describing the Merz reduction process.
STATEMENT submitted by the commissioner of public works of the cost of collection of ashes, garbage and refuse for the past ten years. (Proc. Common Council. 1903, p. 1215-1219.)   * SYA

1908

OPERATING results of the Buffalo refuse utilization plant. 1,200 w., 4 illus. (Engineering record. v. 58, p. 520.)   †† VDA
Light refuse is burned in a Morse-Boulfer furnace and the heat is utilized for generating steam to operate the pumps of the sewage station.

1910

WARD, Francis G. Public health and the public purse. (Report of the 10th annual conference of sanitary officers state of New York. p. 114-118.)   SPA
Collection of ashes, refuse and garbage in Buffalo; general public services most closely allied to the question of public health are collection and disposal of city waste and water supply; report of refuse utilization plant for 1910.

Burnley, England.
See also above General Works, under date of 1904.

1904

MASSEY, J. B. Burnley's new refuse destructor. (Sanitary record. v. 33, p. 126.)   † SPA

Caen, France.

1912

ARRÊTÉ concernant l'enlèvement des immondices et ordures ménagères à l'aide du matériel hygiénique Ritton, le 23 mars, 1912. (Caen. Bulletin municipal de la ville. Année 20, no. 3, p. 273-276.)

Cambridge, England.

1910

BERGER, Ch. L'incinération des ordures ménagères à Cambridge. (La technique sanitaire. Année 5, p. 185-187.)   † SPA
—— Same. (Revue industrielle. v. 41, p. 216.)   †† VA

Cambridge, Mass.
See also above General Works, under the dates of 1896 and 1901, resp.

1911

REPORT, A, to the mayor and city council upon a comprehensive plan for the development and improvement of the streets

Special Cities — Cambridge, cont'd.
and the disposal of refuse. n. p., n. d. 72 p.,
1 map. 8°.
The report is made by a special commission appointed by the mayor in April, 1910. The report
was made in cooperation with the Cambridge Tax-
payers' Assoc. On p. 13 there is a table of comparative statistics of the larger Massachusetts cities,
excluding Boston, relative to population, total valuation, mileage and valuation of streets.

1912

REFUSE disposal in Cambridge, Mass.
2500 w. (Municipal engineer. Feb., 1912.)
VDA

Cambuslang, Scotland.

1908

ELECTRICITY from refuse. 350 w. (Electrical review, London. v. 63, p. 983.)
†† VGA
Cost figures at Cambuslang electricity and destructor works for a 3 month period.

Canton, Ohio.

1901

REPORT on proposed garbage disposal
for Canton. (Ohio. Board of Health.
17 annual report 1901/2, p. 160-161.) **SPB**

Cassel, Germany.

1901

[NOTE on the municipalization on April 1,
1901, of the work of street cleaning, and
house and street refuse removal.] (Deutsche Vierteljahrsschrift für öffentliche Gesundheitspflege. v. 34, suppl. p. 602.)
SPA

Charlottenburg, Germany.
Serial
MÜLLBESEITIGUNG. Bericht, 1907-1910. (In:
Charlottenburg. Verwaltungsbericht, 1907-
1909/10.) *** SYD**
STÄDTISCHE Strassenreinigung. Bericht,
1900-1910. (In: Charlottenburg. Verwaltungsbericht, 1900-1909/10.) *** SYD**
The report for 1900/1 is reproduced in Zeitschrift
für Transportwesen und Strassenbau. Jahrg. 19,
p. 53-55. **†† TPB**
Non-serial
1906
VERSTADTLICHUNG, Die, der Müllabfuhr in
Charlottenburg. (Gesundheits-Ingenieur.
Jahrg. 29, p. 128-129; 194-197.) **†† SPA**
1907
MEYER, Karl M. Die Müllbeseitigung
nach dem Dreiteilungsverfahren in Charlottenburg. (Zeitschrift für Transportwesen und Strassenbau. Jahrg. 24, p. 327-331;
illus.) **†† TPB**
ZUR Neuregelung der Charlottenburger
Müllabfuhr. (Same. Jahrg. 24, p. 123-124,
232.) **†† TPB**
1908
MÜLLABFUHR. (Archiv für Volkswohlfahrt. Jahrg. 2, p. 616-617.) **† SA**
Municipalisation of garbage disposal occurred on
April 1, 1907. Above is an abstract of the report
of the street cleaning department on waste disposal
since its release from private contract.

THIESING, Hans. Neuere Erfahrungen
auf dem Gebiete der Müllbeseitigung. 8800
w., illus. (Gesundheits-Ingenieur. July
25, 1908.) **†† SPA**
VILLE de Charlottenbourg. Ordures ménagères, enlèvement, triage. (Revue pratique d'hygiène municipal. Année 4, p. 549-
550.) **SPA**

Chattanooga, Tenn.
1912
MUNICIPAL record. v. 1. *** SYA**
v. 1., no. 11. March. Fly tight garbage receptacles. v. 1., no. 12. May. Improved street cleaning methods. [Ordinance.] Regulates "dump pick-
ing."

Chelsea, England.
1891
DISPOSAL of household refuse at Chelsea,
England. 1000 w. (Engineering record.
v. 24, p. 250.) **†† VDA**

Chemnitz, Germany.
Serial
DÜNGERABFUHR. Bericht, 1900-1910. (Chem-
nitz. Verwaltungsbericht, 1900-1910.)
*** SYD**
MÜLLABFUHRWESEN. Bericht, 1909-1910.
(Same. 1909-1910.) *** SYD**
REINHALTUNG, Schneebeseitigung, etc. Be-
richt, 1902-1910. (Same, 1902-1910.)
*** SYD**
Non-serial
1900
GRAPHISCHE Darstellung des 10ten Be-
triebsjahres der Chemnitzer-Dünger-Ab-
fuhrgesellschaft über gesammt Arbeitslei-
stung. 1 sheet. (Chemnitz. Verwaltungs-
bericht. 1900, facing p. 316.) *** SYD**
1908
[NOTE on the inauguration of the muni-
cipal refuse removal system.] (Chemnitz.
Verwaltungsbericht. 1908, p. 120.) *** SYD**

Chicago, Ill.
See also above General Works, under the dates of
1891, 1894 and 1911, resp.
Serial
ANNUAL report of the board of public
works, 1-2, 4-9, 11-15. 1862-1863, 1865-1870,
1872-1876. **VDDA**
These reports contain informal returns on street
cleaning. They are continued in the following:
ANNUAL report of the bureau of streets,
1-17. 1876-1892. (In: Chicago. Annual
report of the Public Works Department.
1876-1892.) **VDDA**
Continued as:
ANNUAL report of the bureau of street
cleaning, 1-6. 1893-1898. (In: Same, 1893-
1898.) **VDDA**
Continued as:
ANNUAL report of the bureau of streets,
24-35. 1899-1910. (In: Same, 1899-1910.)
VDDA
The numbering of this series resumes that begun
in 1876. The reports at present include street and
alley cleaning, garbage, ash, rubbish, snow and dead
animal removal.

Special Cities — Chicago, cont'd.

Non-serial

1893

MORSE, W. F. The disposal of the garbage and waste of the World's Columbian Exposition. (American Public Health Assoc. Public health papers and reports. v. 19, p. 53-62.)   **SPA**
—— Same. (Scientific American supplement. v. 36, p. 14992.)   †† **VA**

1897

HOOKER, George E. Cleaning streets by contract — a sidelight from Chicago. (Review of reviews. v. 15, p. 437-441.)   • **DA**
Disapproval of the contract system of street cleaning in Chicago.

1899

REYNOLDS, Arthur R. Garbage disposal tin Chicago1. (Municipal engineering. v. 16, p. 31-33.)   **VDA**
Paper before the American Society of Municipal Improvements, by the commissioner of health of Chicago.

190–

SELFRIDGE, Harry G. Suggestions on the problem of cleaning the streets of Chicago... Chicago: City Homes Assoc. 1190–?1. 12 p. 8°.   **VDH p.v.1, no.4**

1901

UTILIZATION of garbage furnace heat at one of the Chicago electric light plants. 500 w. (Engineering news. v. 45, p. 124.)   †† **VDA**
There is also an editorial of 2000 w.

1903

GARBAGE, The, disposal question in Chicago. (Municipal engineering. v. 25, p. 433-434.)   **VDA**
Synopsis of report of the special garbage commission.

1906

CHICAGO garbage ordinance. Text of art. 12 of the health ordinance. (Municipal engineering. v. 30, p. 34-35.)   **VDA**

1907

STREET cleaning in the central business district of Chicago. (Engineering record. v. 55, p. 625-628.)   †† **VDA**

1908

ALDEN, Emmons J. Chicago garbage reduction plant. 3,500 w., 4 illus. (In Engineering news. v. 59, p. 278.)   †† **VDA**
Process is known as the "drying system." Garbage is crushed to a uniform size, dried at high temperatures, then treated with gasoline, by which the grease is extracted.

NEUE, Die, Müllverwertungsanlage in Chicago. (Zeitschrift für Transportwesen und Strassenbau. Jahrg. 25, p. 251-253.)   †† **TPB**

PERKINS, F. C. Chicago underground railway system of refuse disposal. 900 w. (Municipal engineering. v. 35, p. 21.)   **VDA**

1910

CHICAGO, The, incinerator. A device for destroying rubbish which cannot be burned under a boiler. (Iron age. v. 85, p. 1263; illus.)   †† **VDA**

CHICAGO waste disposal system. 1800 w., illus. (Engineering record. v. 62, p. 8-9.)   †† **VDA**

1912

CITIZENS' Association of Chicago. 1Facts and suggestions in regard to the disposal of the garbage of Chicago.1 4 l. 8°. (Bulletin 28.)   **Room 229**
1NEWSPAPER clippings of May,' 1912.1   **Room 229**

Chiswick, England.

1908

DESTRUCTOR plant for Chiswick urban district council. 900 w., 4 drawings. (Engineering. v. 85, p. 12.)   †† **VDA**

Cincinnati, O.

Serial

ANNUAL report of the street cleaning department, 1891. (In: Cincinnati. Engineering Department. Annual report, 1891.)   • **SYA**
Continued as:
ANNUAL report of the street cleaning department, 1892-1897. (In: Cincinnati. Board of Administration. Annual report, 1892-1897.)   • **SYA**
Continued as:
ANNUAL report of the street cleaning department, 1898-1899. (In: Cincinnati. Board of City Affairs, 1898-1899.)   • **SYA**
Continued as:
ANNUAL report of the street cleaning department, 1900-1909. (In: Cincinnati. Board of Public Service, 1900-1909.)   • **SYA**

Non-serial

1896

GARBAGE utilization at Cincinnati and New Orleans. 5,000 w., 1 drawing. (Engineering news. v. 36, p. 236.)   †† **VDA**
Simonin reduction process in use in both cities. See also editorial, p. 232.

1899

HERRMANN, August. Disposition of garbage at Cincinnati. (Proc. 6. annual convention of the American Society of Municipal Improvements, p. 241-244.)   **SERA**
—— Same, condensed. (Municipal engineering. v. 17, p. 333-335.)   **VDA**
GARBAGE disposal at Cincinnati. 700 w. (Engineering record. v. 40, p. 465.)   †† **VDA**
Abstract of report by August Herrmann, giving history of the contract for garbage disposal at Cincinnati.

1900

NOTES on garbage disposal at Cincinnati, O. 1,200 w. (Engineering news. v. 43, p. 271.)   †† **VDA**
Simonin reduction process used with little offense.

1902

STANTON, Byron. Report upon the disposal of refuse materials in Cincinnati, O., from 1872 to 1902. (American Public Health Assoc. Public health papers and reports. v. 28, p. 59-63.)   **SPA**

Special Cities — Cincinnati, cont'd.

1904

CINCINNATI'S exclusive garbage contract ordinance. (Municipal engineering. v. 26, p. 182.)   **VDA**
Synopsis of decision of Circuit Court at Cincinnati, Jan. 19, 1903, declaring the ordinance invalid.

1912

ɪNEWSPAPER clippings of June, 1912.ɪ
Room 229

Cleckheaton, England.
See above, General Works, under date of 1904.

Cleveland, O.
See also above General Works, under the dates of 1909 and 1911, resp.

Serial

ANNUAL report of the superintendent of streets, 1-2, 4, 8-11. 1891-1892, 1894, 1898-1902. (ɪn: Cleveland. Department of Public Works. Annual report, 1891-1892, 1894, 1898-1902.)   **VDDA**
—— Same. 1891-1892, 1894-1895, 1897-1902. (ɪn: Same. Collected document edition.)   **＊SYA**
The work of street cleaning was assigned to a separate division in 1903.
ANNUAL report of the division of street cleaning, 1903-1909. (ɪn: Cleveland. Public Service Board. Department of Streets. 1903-1909.)   **＊SYA**
ANNUAL report of the garbage disposal plant, 1-5. 1905-1909. (ɪn: Cleveland. Public Service Board. Department of Streets. 1905-1909.)   **＊SYA**

Non-serial

1876

WELLS, Frank. Filth in its relation to disease. A report made to the board of police commissioners of the city of Cleveland. ɪCleveland: Leader Prtg. Co., 1876.ɪ 2 p.l., 163 p., 4 pl.   **SPL**
Pages 130–131 only relate to garbage.

1900

GARBAGE reduction at Cleveland, O. 1,400 w., 3 illus. (Engineering news. v. 43, p. 358.)   **†† VDA**
Garbage is digested with steam and the tankage pressed and dried. Grease is extracted by the steam.

1906

STREET cleaning methods in Cleveland. (Municipal engineering. v. 31, p. 437-438.)   **VDA**

1907

Two years' operations of the municipal garbage reduction works, Cleveland, O. 4,000 w. (Engineering news. v. 57, p. 487.)   **†† VDA**
Contains valuable cost data.

1908

CLEVELAND, O., garbage reduction works. 2,500 w., 1 drawing, 2 illus. (Engineering record. v. 57, p. 659.)   **†† VDA**
GARBAGE collection and disposal at Cleveland. 1,800 w., 1 drawing, 11 illus. (City hall. v. 10, p. 55.)   **†† SER**

—— Same. (Domestic engineering. Oct. 3, 1908.)   **† VEWA**
GARBAGE disposal at Cleveland. 1,100 w. (Municipal journal and engineer. v. 25, p. 418.)   **†† SER**
Description of improved dryer and new type of percolator in use.

1911

GREGORY, John H. Operating results of the garbage reduction works of Cleveland and Columbus, O. 3000 w. (Engineering news. Nov. 30, 1911.)   **†† VDA**

Coblenz, Germany.
See also above General Works, under date of 1908.
ABFUHR und Strassenreinigung, 1905-1910. (ɪn: Coblenz. Verwaltungsbericht, 1905-1910.)   **＊SYD**

Colne, England.
See above General Works, under date of 1901.

Cologne, Germany.
See also above General Works, under date of 1907.

Serial

FUHRPARK, Strassenreinigung und Strassenberieselung. Bericht, 1906. (ɪn: Cöln. Bericht und Stand der Gemeindeangelegenheiten, 1906.)   **＊SYD**
An abstract of the report for 1900 is printed in Zeitschrift für Transportwesen und Strassenbau. Jahrg. 18, p. 198–199, 456–457.   **†† TPB**

Non-serial

1898

See above Brussels, this date.

1899

ɪTEXT of police regulation of Jan. 19, 1899, and of a mayoral notice relative to household waste removal.ɪ (Centralblatt für allgemeine Gesundheitspflege. v. 18, p. 183-184.)   **SPA**

1906

MÜLLBESEITIGUNGS-VERFAHREN der Maschinenbau-Anstalt Humboldt, Kalk bei Cöln. (Zeitschrift für Transportwesen und Strassenbau. Jahrg. 23, p. 227-231, illus.)   **†† TPB**
VERFAHREN zur Aufbereitung des Hausmülls und Strassenkehrichts. (Same. Jahrg. 23, p. 26-27, illus.)   **†† TPB**
The Humboldt plant, Kalk (Cologne a. R.).

1910

ADAM. Toilette et propreté des rues à Cologne. (Revue d'hygiène et de police sanitaire. v. 32, p. 901-903.)   **SPA**
Ch. 6, of part 3 of an extended article "L'assainissement de Copenhague, de Düsseldorf et de Cologne."

Colombo, Ceylon.

1912

KILMISTER, Clive H. Colombo's refuse destructor. 3500 w., illus. (Surveyor. April 12, 1912.)   **†† VDA**

Colorado Springs, Colo.
REPORT of the health department. 1897-98, 1904-1909, 1910, June, 1911-1912.   **† SDN**
Each number contains a report on the city dump and on city scavenging. The report on the removal

Special Cities — Colorado Springs, cont'd.
of dead animals was begun in April 1905, and that on the city dump and scavenging was begun some time between Dec. 1909 and June 1910.

Columbus, O.
1900
GARBAGE reduction at Columbus, O. 2,200 w. (Engineering news. v. 44, p. 47.)
†† **VDA**
Method of collection and reduction described.
1906
NOTABLE report on garbage and refuse collection and refuse disposal at Columbus, O. 3,300 w. (Engineering news. v. 55, p. 304.)
†† **VDA**
Review of report prepared by experts, giving estimates and recommendations.
1910
COLUMBUS garbage reduction plant. First municipally conducted destruction plant in the world. 1450 w., illus. (Municipal journal and engineer. v. 28, p. 393-395.)
†† **SER**
MUNICIPAL, The, garbage reduction plant at Columbus, O. (Municipal engineering.
†† **VDA**
1911
GARBAGE reduction at Columbus. Operation of municipal plant of 80 tons capacity; etc. 5000 w. (Municipal journal and engineer. v. 31, p. 622.)
†† **SER**
TRAITEMENT, Le, des ordures ménagères par digestion dans la vapeur, à Columbus, O. (Le Génie civil. v. 59, p. 52-54; 1 pl.)
†† **VA**
MUNICIPAL, The, garbage reduction plant at Columbus, O. (Municipal engineering. v. 40, p. 322-327; illus.)
VDA
SIX months' financial operating results of the garbage reduction plant of Columbus, O. 1000 w. (Engineering news. Oct. 26, 1911.)
†† **VDA**

Copenhagen, Denmark.
1891
MEYERS, J. F. Experiments in the burning of house refuse. (Transactions 7th International Congress of Hygiene and Demography. v. 7, p. 205-210.)   **SPA**
1907
STRASSENREINIGUNG in Kopenhagen. (Zeitschrift für Transportwesen und Strassenbau. Jahrg. 24, p. 494; illus.)   †† **TPB**

Darwen, England.
See above, General Works under date of 1904.

Davenport, Iowa.
1911
GARBAGE disposal by burial. 560 w. (Municipal journal and engineer. v. 31, p. 38.)
†† **SER**

Dayton, O.
See also above the General Works, under date of 1911.
1897
COMMENTS on cremation of garbage at Dayton. (Ohio sanitary bulletin (qr. ser.), v. 1, no. 11.)   **SPB**

Denver, Colo.
Serial
DENVER municipal facts. v. 1-4. 1909-1912.   *SYA
Contains monthly reports on cost of street cleaning. v. 4, no. 19 (May 11, 1912) contains an illustrated article on the 1912 civic parade showing several pictures of sprinkling cart squads, hand sweepers and street cleaning machines. no. 24 (June 15, 1912) publishes tersely some facts on the cost of street and alley cleaning in Denver.

Non-serial
• 1902
DENVER garbage ordinance legal. (Municipal engineering. v. 22, p. 252.)   **VDA**
Synopsis of decision of the District Court, Denver, of March 17, 1902.
1905
NEUE, Eine, Maschine zum Verdichten von Schnee. (Zeitschrift für Transportwesen und Strassenbau. Jahrg. 22, p. 472; illus.)   †† **TPB**
The Farquhar (Denver) snow press.
NEUES, Ein, System von Strassenkehrmaschinen. (Same. Jahrg. 22, p. 473-474.)   †† **TPB**
The Clough (Denver) street sweeper.

Detroit, Mich.
See also above the General Works, under date of 1894.
See also the more recent reports of the Detroit Health Board which all contain recommendations for an improved street and alley scavenger service.
1892
PROBST, C. O. Report on disposal of garbage at Detroit. (Ohio. Board of Health. 8. annual report 1892/3, p. 86-87.)   **SPB**
1898
KEMPSTER, Walter. Garbage disposal in Detroit. (Municipal engineering. v. 15, p. 159-160.)   **VDA**
Extract from the annual report of the health commissioner of Milwaukee.
1903
DETROIT to regulate collection of garbage. (Municipal engineering. v. 25, p. 30-31.)
VDA
Text of decision upholding right of city to contract for removal of garbage.
1906
See also below Rochester. 1906.
GARBAGE disposal in Detroit. (Municipal engineering. v. 31, p. 436-437.)   **VDA**
1909
STREET cleaning in Detroit. (Municipal engineering. v. 36, p. 383-384.)   **VDA**
1910
COMMUNICATION from the Board of Health to the Common Council recommending the erection of one or more rubbish incinerating plants. (Detroit. Journal of the Common Council. 1911, p. 81.)
*SYA
1911
REPORT of special committee on ways and means and ordinances recommending appointment of a joint committee of the Board of Commerce and the Common Coun-

Special Cities — Detroit, cont'd.

cil to inspect the garbage collection and disposal methods of Cleveland, Columbus, Milwaukee and Minneapolis. (Detroit. Journal of the Common Council. 1911, p. 1825.)   **SYA**

Dresden, Germany.
See also above the General Works, under date of 1884.

Serial
BERICHT des Strassenreinigungsamts, 1882-1887, 1889-1903, 1904/8.   **SYD**
These are included in the Verwaltungsbericht des Rathes, etc. The early years contain references to street sprinkling only, later also to street cleaning and at present refuse collection and removal and snow removal are included. The reports for 1895 and 1897 are reproduced in Zeitschrift für Transportwesen und Strassenbau, v. 14 and 16 resp.   ††TPB

Non-serial
1907
STREET cleaning apparatus in Dresden, Germany. (Municipal engineering. v. 33, p. 384-385; 1 illus.)   **VDA**

1911
NIEDNER, Franz. Die Strassenreinigung in den deutschen Städten unter besonderer Berücksichtigung der Dresdener Strassenreinigung. Leipzig, 1911. 2 p.l., 99 p., 5 pl. 4°.   **VDH**

Dublin, Ireland.
See also above the General Works, under date of 1899.

1885
YOUNG, James. On public cleansing. (Journal Sanitary Institute. v. 6, p. 229-239.)   **SPA**
Regarding the scavenging of Dublin.

1905
ALLAN, Fred J. Dublin's new scheme of refuse disposal. (Sanitary record. v. 36, p. 167-168.)   †**SPA**

Duisburg, Germany.
1911
STRASSEN-POLIZEI-ORDNUNG für die Stadtgemeinde Duisburg. Nov. 20, 1911. (Sammlung von Bekanntmachungen und Verordnungen der Stadt. Jahrg. 2, no. 3, p. 58-62.)   **SYA**

Duluth, Minn.
See also above the General Works, under date of 1911.

1906
TEST of the new Decarie garbage incinerator at Duluth [Minn.]. 400 w. (Municipal engineering. v. 30, p. 235.)   **VDA**
From Duluth "News-tribune."

Dunoon, Scotland.
1906
NEW refuse destructor at Dunoon. (Sanitary record. v. 38, p. 544.)   †**SPA**
REFUSE destructor opened at Dunoon [on Nov. 3, 1906]. (County and municipal record. v. 8, p. 91-92.)   ††**SPA**

Düsseldorf, Germany.
Serial
FUHRPARK und Strassenreinigung, 1898-1910/11. (In: Düsseldorf. Bericht über den Stand der Verwaltung. 1898-1910/11.)   **SYD**

Non-serial
1910
BRIX. Nettoyage des rues et enlèvement des immondices [de Düsseldorf]. (Revue d'hygiène et de police sanitaire. v. 32, p. 696-697.)   **SPA**
Ch. 5, of part 2, of an extended article "L'assainissement de Copenhague, de Düsseldorf et de Cologne. By Ed. Imbeaux and R. André.

Ealing, England.
See above the General Works, under date of 1898.

East Orange, N. J.
1907
REPORT on a combined refuse destructor and electric lighting plant for East Orange, N. J. 2,000 w. (Engineering news. v. 57, p. 101.)   ††**VDA**
Review of report, giving estimated costs. See also editorial, p. 109.
WASTE disposal for East Orange [N. J.]. 1,600 w., 3 diagr. (Municipal journal and engineer. v. 22, p. 306.)   ††**SER**
Review of report of committee recommending incineration of mixed garbage and refuse. Consideration of fuel value of waste.

East Providence, R. I.
1911
TEXT of chap. 30 of an ordinance for the care and disposal of garbage and refuse; Aug. 2. (U. S. Public Health and Marine Hospital Service. Public health reports. v. 27, p. 805.)   **SPB**

Eastbourne, England.
1907
DESCRIPTION of refuse destructor at Eastbourne. (Journal sanitary institute. v. 28, p. 214.)   **SPA**

Easton, Penn.
1910
MCNEAL, John. Easton garbage incinerator. illus. (Municipal journal and engineer. v. 29, p. 881-882.).   ††**SER**

Edinburgh, Scotland.
See also above the General Works, under the dates of 1899, 1902 and 1903.
1893
REFUSE destruction at Edinburgh. 2,800 w., 8 drawings, 1 illus. (Engineer, London. v. 86, p. 200.)   ††**VDA**
Horsefall furnace in satisfactory operation.
REFUSE disposal in Edinburgh. 1,100 w. (Engineering record. v. 38, p. 199.)   ††**VDA**
Unsatisfactory results obtained from cremation of refuse.
1904
EDINBURGH inspector of cleansing and lighting. Annual report. (County and municipal record. v. 4, p. 58.)   **SPA**
Review of annual report.

Special Cities — Edinburgh, cont'd.

1908

MacKay, G. A. D. The Edinburgh corporation's cleaning department. (Public works. v. 9, p. 103-107.)   †VDA

Edmonton, Canada.

1909

Whitelaw, T. H. Disposal of city wastes and consideration of nuisances in Edmonton, Alberta, Canada. (American Public Health Assoc. Public health papers and reports. v. 35, part 1, p. 542-545; American journal public hygiene. v. 20, p. 275-278.)   SPA

Essen, Germany.
See above the General Works, under the date of 1897.

Evanston, Ill.

1901

Garbage cremation at Evanston, Ill. 600 w., 3 drawings. (Engineering record. v. 43, p. 553.)   ††VDA

Evansville, Ind.
Annual report of the board of public works, 1894-1896, 1902, 1906-191. (In: Annual reports of the city of Evansville.)   *SYA
All the reports contain returns of street sweeping and sprinkling, and since 1896 there is a return each year of the operations of the crematory. There is also material in the reports of the Board of Health relative to the crematory which is managed jointly by the Board of Public Works and by the Board of Health.

Fall River, Mass.
Annual report of the street department, 1897-1911. (In: Annual reports of the city of Fall River.)   *SYA
It is only since 1897 that these reports regularly contain returns relative to street cleaning and scavenger service.

Findlay, O.

1892

Carrothers, M. M. Cremation of night soil and garbage at Findlay, Ohio. 1800 w. (Annals of hygiene. v. 7, p. 153.)   SPA
Engle cremator; gas used as fuel.

Fiume, Hungary.
See above the General Works, under date of 1907.

Fort Leavenworth, Kansas.
See above the General Works, under date of 1905.

Fort Wayne, Indiana.

1900

Scherer, H. P. How properly to collect and dispose of garbage. (Municipal engineering. v. 19, p. 331-335.)   VDA
Written by the mayor of Fort Wayne, Ind. and relates largely to that city.

Frankfurt a. M., Germany.
See also above the General Works, under dates of 1909 and 1910.

Serial
Bericht des Magistrats die Verwaltung betreffend, 1881, 1883, 1886-1893, 1906-1908.   *SYD
Contains reports on street cleaning and refuse removal, and, in the more recent years, on refuse incineration.

Non-serial

1898

See above Brussels, this date.

Freiburg, Germany.
See above the General Works, under date of 1898.

Fulham, England.
See below, London.

Fürth, Germany.

1911

Städtisches technisches Betriebsamt. Müllabfuhr und Müllverbrennung in der Stadt Fürth. (Gesundheits-Ingenieur. Jahrg. 34, p. 655-656; 7 illus.)   ††SPA

Geneva, Switzerland.

1899

Wagnon, Ami. [Report on sanitation of towns by refuse incineration.]
M. Wagnon was president of the conseil d'administration of Geneva. The original of the report is not, at this time, in the Library.
—— Same, reviewed. (Electrical review, London. 1899, p. 779-780.)   ††VGA

Genoa, Italy.

1900

Capitolato d'appalto pei servizi della spazzatura, della bagnatura, della lavatura, rimozione della neve, ecc. nel territorio de comune di Genova. Genova, 1900. 39 p. pap. f°.

1905

Resoconto morale della giunta municipale [del] minicipio di Genova per l'esercizio 1905. Genova, 1906. 649 p. 4°.   *SYF
Pages 213-215, "Sgombro e nettezza della vie e piazze pubbliche," relate to provisions for street cleaning and refuse removal upon the expiration of the Pereno contract of 1900, listed above.

Glasgow, Scotland.
See also above General Works, under the dates of 1888, 1898, 1902 and 1904.

Serial
Statement of the revenue and expenditure of the cleansing department for year ended May 31, 1895-1897, 1899-1900.   TIB p.box
A review of the report for 1909 is printed in County and municipal record. v. 13, p. 458-459.   SPA

Non-serial

1897

Murdoch. The treatment and utilisation of refuse from the city of Glasgow.
The original, which appeared in the Journal of state medicine, Nov. 1897, p. 502, is not, at this time, in the Library.
—— Same, reviewed. (Revue d'hygiène et de police sanitaire. v. 20, p. 665-667.)   SPA

Special Cities — Glasgow, cont'd.

1906

McColl, D. The cleansing of Glasgow. (County and municipal record. v. 7, p. 310-312.) **SPA**

1907

Cleansing in Glasgow. (County and municipal record. v. 8, p. 450.)
Brief summary of systems from 1800–1868.

1908

Farming as a department of cleansing. (County and municipal record. v. 11, p. 355.) **SPA**
The cleansing department of the city of Glasgow owns various farming areas, comprising 1508 acres of arable land. The above note describes Ryding estate, near Coatbridge, consisting of seven farms.

1909

Chalmers, A. K. The functions of a cleansing department in relation to public health administration. (County and municipal record. v. 13, p. 194-196.) **SPA**
Paper read at the annual conference of cleansing superintendents, held at Glasgow, June, 1908. Relates to Glasgow only.

Gorton, England.

1905

Refuse destructor for the urban district council of Gorton. (Sanitary record. v. 35, p. 291.) † **SPA**

Govan, Scotland.
See above: General Works under date of 1902.

Grand Rapids, Mich.
See also above General Works, under the dates of 1904 and 1911.

1906

See also below Rochester, 1906.
Grand Rapids garbage problem. 800 w. (Municipal journal and engineer. v. 20, p. 329.) †† **SER**
Reviews report of commission of investigation concerning best method for disposal of garbage.

1911

Grand Rapids garbage disposal. 500 w. (Municipal journal and engineer. v. 31, p. 498.) †† **SER**

Greenock, England.

1906

Proposed destructor for Greenock. (County and municipal record. v. 6, p. 406.) **SPA**

1908

Combined electricity works and destructor station at Greenock. 2,500 w., 3 drawings, 3 illus. (Electrical engineering, London. v. 3, p. 263.) †† **VGA**
Combined refuse destructor and electrical generating station in England. 1,800 w., 1 drawing. (Engineering record. v. 57, p. 726.) †† **VDA**
Description of plant at Greenock.
Greenock electricity department; opening of new refuse destructor station. 2500 w., 6 illus. (Electrical engineer, London. v. 47, p. 224.) †† **VGA**

Improvements in refuse destruction. 2,400 w. (Canadian engineer. v. 15, p. 248.) **VDA**
Description of combined plant at Greenock, Eng.
Refuse destructor and electricity generating station at Greenock. 2,500 w., 1 drawing, 10 illus. (Engineer, London, v. 105, p. 471.) †† **VDA**
Zwei neue englische Anlagen über die Verbrennung städtischer Abfallstoffe. (Zeitschrift für Transportwesen und Strassenbau. Jahrg. 25, p. 183-186; 1 illus.) †† **TPB**
Greenock and Chiswick.

Grimsby, England.

1903

Grimsby's new refuse destructor. (Sanitary record. v. 31, p. 575-576.) † **SPA**

Groningen, Netherlands.

1638

Verclaringe over de ordonnantie van't reyningen der straten. Gemaeckt ende gearresteert den 17. Feb. 1638. Groningen: H. Sas, 1638. 2 l. 4°.

1668

Ordonnantie op het reynigen der stadts merckten en straeten binnen Groningen. [Also] Additionalen by die hijr voorstaende ordonnantie... Groningen: F. Bronchorst, 1668. [1669.] 7 l. 4°.

1679

Ordonnantie...op het schoon-houden van straten, merckten, kerck-hoven, bruggen, werven, wedden ende andere publieke plaetsen, mitsgaden dependentien van dien. Gepubliceert...t'Utrecht den 17. Juny 1639 ende gerenoveert met eenige veranderinge op den 19. Nov. 1674. Utrecht: W. van Paddenburgh, 1679. 8 l. 4°.

1699

Ordonnantie [regarding the disposition of street manure in the city of Groningen]. Groningen: C. Barlinck-Hof, 1699. 6 l. 4°.

Guildford, England.

1910

Mason, C. G. New refuse detructor and sewage ejector works in Guildford. 7700 w. (Proc. Institute of Municipal and County Engineers. v. 37, p. 266.) **VDA**
— Same. (County and municipal record. v. 16, p. 84-88.) **SPA**

Hackney, England.
See below, London.

Hague, The, Holland.
Bergsma, G. H. E. De electrische motor-sproeiwagen der openbare reiniging te 's Gravenhage. 2000 w. (De Ingenieur. July 10, 1909.) †† **VDA**

Hamburg, Germany.
See also above the General Works, under the dates of 1896, 1903, 1907 and 1909.

1894

Reinicke, and Andreas Meyer. Beseitigung des Kehrichts und anderer städtischer Abfälle, besonders durch Verbrennung.

Special Cities — Hamburg, cont'd.
(Deutsche Vierteljahrsschrift für öffentliche Gesundheitspflege. v. 27, p. 11-35; illus.)   **SPA**
Relates chiefly to Hamburg and Berlin.

1896

MEYER, F. Andreas. Die städtische Verbrennungsanstalt für Abfallstoffe am Bulleerdeich in Hamburg. (Deutsche Vierteljahrsschrift für öffentliche Gesundheitspflege. v. 29, p. 353-378; 9 illus.)   **SPB**
—— Same, reviewed. Gesundheitsingenieur. Jahrg. 20, p. 398-400.)   †† **SPA**
—— Same, reviewed. (Minutes Proc. Institute of Civil Engineers. v. 129, p. 434.)   **VDA**
—— Same, reviewed. (Zeitschrift für Transportwesen und Strassenbau. Jahrg. 15, p. 23-25.)   †† **TPB**

1897

HERING, Rudolph. Disposal of garbage and refuse; construction, cost and operation of Hamburgh, Germany, works. 4,500 w., 15 drawings, 2 illus. (Engineering record. v. 36, p. 446.)   †† **VDA**
Horsefall furnaces in operation over 16 months; see also editorial, p. 441.

1905

VERBRENNUNGANSTALT für Abfallstoffe in Hamburg. (Zeitschrift für Transportwesen und Strassenbau. Jahrg. 22, p. 59.)   †† **TPB**

1906

NEUES, Ein, Verfahren zur Trennung des Hausmülls oder ähnlichen Sammelguts in seine Bestandtheile. (Zeitschrift für Transportwesen und Strassenbau. Jahrg. 23, p. 512-513; illus.)   †† **TPB**
The Lodde (Hamburg) separator.

1910

GARBAGE disposal in Hamburg. 500 w. (Municipal journal and engineer. v. 29, p. 739.)   †† **SER**

Havre, France.
See above the General Works, under date of 1884.

Hawick, England.
See above the General Works, under date of 1898.

Hereford, England.
See above the General Works, under date of 1904.

Holland, Mich.

1911

TEXT of regulations of the Board of Health for the disposal of garbage and refuse; Oct. 2. (United States. Public Health and Marine Hospital Service. Public health reports. v. 27, p. 963.)   **SPB**

Houston, Texas.

Serial

ANNUAL report of the city scavenger, 1903-1911. (In: Mayor's annual message and department reports, 1903-1911.) * **SYA**
ANNUAL report of the superintendent of garbage, 1903-1911. (In: Same. 1903-1911.)   * **SYA**

Non-serial
1910

GARBAGE cremation (in the city of Houston, Texas). (Municipal engineering. v. 38, p. 63.)   **VDA**

1911

DULLER, David M. The garbage crematory at Houston, Texas. (Municipal engineering. v. 40, p.177-180; illus.)   **VDA**
REFUSE crematory at Houston. illus. (Municipal journal and engineer. v. 30, p. 84-85.)   †† **SER**

Hull, England.

1905

ATKINSON, Peter. The destruction and utilisation of town refuse (pertaining especially to Hull). (Sanitary record. v. 36, p. 325-326.)   † **SPA**

Ilkley, England.

1905

HORSFALL destructor at Ilkley. (Sanitary record. v. 36, p. 524-525; illus.) † **SPA**

Indianapolis, Ind.

Serial

ANNUAL report of the street sweeping and sprinkling department, 1-5. 1905-1909. (In: Indianapolis. Public Works Department. Annual report, 15-19. 1905-1909.)   **VDDA**

Non-serial
1901

GARBAGE disposal at Indianapolis, Ind. 1,600 w. (Engineering news. v. 45, p. 83.)   †† **VDA**
History and brief description of reduction process in use.
STREET cleaning specifications for Indianapolis and San Francisco. (Municipal engineering. v. 20, p. 74-76.)   **VDA**

1905

STREET cleaning equipment (of Indianapolis, Ind.). (Municipal engineering. v. 28, p. 486; 1 illus.)   **VDA**

Issy-les-Moulineaux, France.

1908

USINE de broyage et d'incinération des ordures ménagères. 1500 w. illus. (La nature. v. 70, p. 369.)   **OA**
Disposal of refuse at Issy-les-Moulineaux; part of refuse is ground up for fertilizer and part is cremated.

Ivry-sur-Seine, France.

1910

CONSEIL d'Hygiène Publique et de Salubrité du Département de la Seine. Traitement des ordures ménagères. (La Technique sanitaire. Année 5, p. 182-185.)   † **SPA**
Discussion at the session of May 13, 1910, of the report of M. Henriot on the installation of a refuse destructor plant at Ivry-sur-Seine.

Special Cities, cont'd.

Ixelles, Belgium.

1909

USINE d'incinération d'Ixelles. Essais de la puissance de combustion et calorifique des fours destructeurs d'immondices. (La Technique sanitaire. Année 4 (suppl.), p. 64-65.) † SPA

Kingstown, Ireland.

1907

KINGSTOWN refuse destructor. (Sanitary record. v. 39, p. 123.) † SPA

La Crosse, Wis.

1910

FALK, George. Street cleaning in La Crosse. 550 w. (Municipal journal and engineer. v. 29, p. 426.) †† SER

SOME street details. Templates, bulletin boards, hand sweeper carts, waste receptacles. 2000 w., illus. (Same. v. 29, p. 507.) †† SER

Lafayette, Ind.

1901

BURRAGE, Severance. Garbage disposal in Lafayette, Indiana. (Municipal engineering. v. 20, p. 329-334; illus.) VDA

Leeds, England.
See also above the General Works, under dates of 1888 and 1896.

1881

DESTRUCTION of garbage by fire. 1800 w., 2 drawings. (Sanitary engineer. v. 4, p. 164.) VDA
Based on report of the medical officer of Saint Pancras, Eng., describing the Fryer carbonizer and destructor in use at Leeds.

1882

STAGG, Charles. The burning of town refuse at Leeds. (Minutes of Proc. Institution of Civil Engineers. v. 68, p. 290-294; illus.) VDA
—— Same, condensed. (Sanitary engineer. v. 6, p. 291.) VDA

Leicester, England.

1903

ALLEN, F. W. Collection, disposal and utilization of town refuse in Leicester. 7000 w. (Journal Sanitary Institute. v. 25, p. 1.) SPA

Leipzig, Germany.
See also above, the General Works, under date of 1898.
STRASSENREINIGUNGSWESEN, 1884-1908. (In: Leipzig. Verwaltungsbericht, 1884-1908.) ' STD

Leith, Scotland.
See also above the General Works, under date of 1904.

1902

WHY refuse destructors are essential (to Leith). (Sanitary record. v. 30, p. 41.) † SPA

1910

REFUSE problem in Leith. (County and municipal record. v. 15, p. 38.) SPA
Extract from annual report of medical officer Dr. Robertson.

Lewisham, England.
See below, London.

Lexington, Ky.
See below Rochester under date of 1906.

Leyton, England.
See also above, the General Works, under date of 1898.

1896

REFUSE destructor at Leyton. 1,300 w., 5 drawings. (Engineering. v. 62, p. 671.) VDA
First destructor of its kind in England successful in burning pressed sludge mixed with refuse.

1898

LEYTON sewage and destruction works. 1,300 w., 2 drawings, 1 illus. (Engineer, London. v. 85, p. 115.) †† VDA
House refuse and sewage sludge are cremated. Considerable power is produced.

TEST of a refuse crematory. 900 w., 1 drawing. (Engineering record. v. 37, p. 299.) †† VDA
Test at Leyton, Eng. of refuse mixed with pressed sewage sludge. Favorable results were obtained. See also editorial, p. 291.

Lille, France.
See above, the General Works, under date of 1884.

Little Rock, Ark.

1911

TEXT of ordinance no. 1720 for the collection and disposal of refuse; Oct. 2. (U. S. Public Health and Marine Hospital Service. Public health reports. v. 27, p. 964.) SPB

Liverpool, England.
See also above, the General Works, under date of 1896 and 1904.

1907

HOUSE refuse: collection and disposal. 1200 w. (Journal of the Sanitary Institute. v. 29, p. 176.) SPA
Relates chiefly to conditions in Liverpool in 1907.

1911

HORSFALL destructor; Mersey docks. 3000 w., illus. (Engineering. Nov. 17, 1911.) VDA

London, England.
See also above, the General Works, under dates of 1884, 1891, 1894, 1898 and 1899.

Serial

LONDON statistics, v. 7-21. 1896/7-1910-/11. SDG
Before 1896/7 these volumes contain no material relative to the subjects of this list. From 1896/7 to date there is material on street cleansing, scavenging and watering and, in recent years, snow removal is included. Beginning with 1903/4 there are tables relative to refuse destructors and, from 1906-/7, relative to refuse collection and disposal.
The annual report of the London County Council should also be used by those interested.

Special Cities — London, cont'd.

Non-serial

1817

GREAT BRITAIN. An Act for better paving, improving and regulating the streets of the metropolis, and removing and preventing nuisances and obstructions therein. Passed June 16, 1817. London, 1820. 228 p. 8°.   **VDH**

1843

COCHRANE, Charles. On the present state of the streets of the metropolis, and the importance of their amelioration. (Minutes of Proc. Institution of Civil Engineers. v. 2, p. 202-203.)   **VDA**

1851

HAYWOOD, William. Report to the committee for general purposes of the commissioners of sewers of London upon street cleansing. London, ₁1851?₁. 50 p., 3 foldg. pl. 8°.   **SB p.v.2**

1873

FOSTER, P. Le Neve. Report on the application of science and art to street-paving and street-cleaning of the metropolis. ₁With appendices.₁ n. t.-p. ₁London, 1873?₁ 34 p. 8°.   **VDH p.box 1**

1885

EASSIE, W. Collection and disposal of house refuse. 3100 w. (Journal of the Sanitary Institute. v. 6, p. 223.)   **SPA**
London and Paris methods described.

1894

FRESH from English roads. (Social economist. v. 7, p. 193-198.)   **TAA**
Street cleanliness, comparison between London and New York.

1895

MASON, Charles. Scavenging, disposal of refuse. 7200 w. (Journal of the Sanitary Institute. v. 16, p. 464.)   **SPA**
Relates largely to London under the Public Health London (1891) Act.

1898

See above under Brussels, this date.

1901

BLASHILL, T. The state of London streets. (Journal of the Sanitary Institute. v. 22, p. 6-23.)   **SPA**

1906

DAMPFMOTORWAGEN für städtische Zwecke. Kombiniert für Wasser- und Mülltransport. (Zeitschrift für Transportwesen und Strassenbau. Jahrg. 23, p. 159-160; illus.)
The London refuse removal motor truck.

1907

LONDON's municipal electric plants. 500 w. (Municipal journal and engineer. v. 22, p. 585.)   **†† SER**
Statement of expenditures and returns from destructive plants.

1908

LONDON County Council. By-laws and regulations. Revised to Feb. 1908. 506 p. 8°.   **✱SYA**
Contains by-laws relative to refuse removal.

1911

THOMSON, Lyon. The collection and disposal of house and trade refuse. 2200 w. (Journal of the Sanitary Institute. v. 32, p. 57.)   **SPA**

FULHAM

See also above, the General Works, under dates of 1901 and 1904.

1901

ENGLISH combined central station and destructor plant. 4,400 w., 3 drawings, 5 illus. (Electrical world. v. 37, p. 705.)   **†† VGA**
Description of plant at Fulham, London.

1906

FULHAM refuse destructor. (Sanitary record. v. 38, p. 39.)   **† SPA**
—— Same. (County and municipal record. v. 6, p. 295.)   **SPA**

1908

PERKINS, Frank C. Destructor electric plant. 800 w., 1 drawing, 3 illus. (National engineer. v. 12, p. 496.)   **† VFA**
Description of destructor at Fulham, London, combined with electric light and power plants.

HACKNEY

1904

ELECTRICITY works and destructor of the metropolitan borough of Hackney. 1500 w., 1 drawing, 6 illus. (Electrical review, London. v. 54, p. 423.)   **†† VGA**
ROBINSON, Leonard L. Hackney municipal electricity and destructor works. (Public works. v. 3, p. 352-360.)   **† VDA**

LEWISHAM

1897

WILLOUGHBY refuse destructor. 800 w., 2 drawings. (Engineer, London. v. 84, p. 271.)   **†† VDA**
Destructor is operated at Lewisham, Eng.

ST. PANCRAS

1900

BLAIR, W. Nisbet. The insanitary condition of London streets. (Journal of the Sanitary Institute. v. 21, p. 289-307.)   **SPA**
—— Same, condensed. (Municipal engineering. v. 18, p. 266-267.)   **VDA**
—— Same, reviewed. (Engineering record. v. 41, p. 222.)   **†† VDA**
—— Same review translated. (Zeitschrift für Transportwesen und Strassenbau. Jahrg. 17, p. 231-232.)   **†† TPB**
The original article is based largely on experiences in the parish of St. Pancras.

SHOREDITCH

See also above, the General Works, under date of 1898.

1897

PERRY, Nelson W. Electric light from city refuse. (Cassier's magazine. v. 13, p. 99-112; illus.)   **VDA**
The Shoreditch works.
REFUSE and light. 2,500 w. (Engineering. v. 64, p. 19.)   **†† VDA**
Editorial commendation of the combined refuse destruction and electric-lighting plant at Shoreditch, London.

Special Cities — London, cont'd.

1898

Scott, Ernest K. Combined destructor and electric light plants. 1,200 w. (Electrical review, London. v. 43, p. 856.)
†† **VGA**
Shoreditch plant, London. See also editorial, p. 849.

1899

Russell, Charles Newton. Combined refuse-destructors and power plants. 22 p., 3 diagr., 6 drawings. (Minutes of Proc. of Institution of Civil Engineers. v. 139, p. 181.) **VDA**
Discussion, 43 p. Results from the plant at Shoreditch, London.

1904

Russell, Charles N. Refuse destruction by burning, and the utilization of heat generated. 5,500 w., 1 diagr., 7 drawings. (Transactions of the American Society of Mechanical Engineers, v. 25, p. 982.) **VDA**
Discussion, 3,600 w.
—— Same. (Proceedings of the Institution of Mechanical Engineers. v. 67, p. 591.) **VFA**
—— Same, condensed. 3,200 w. (Municipal engineering. v. 27, p. 39.) **VDA**.
Shoreditch plant, London, and its operation.

WANDSWORTH
See also above, the General Works, under date of 1904.
House refuse dispute [at Wandsworth; synopsis of judgment rendered in the King's Bench Division]. (Sanitary record. v. 38, p. 59.) † **SPA**
See also the editorial on p. 52.

Los Angeles, Cal.
See also below, San Francisco, the serial group.

1912

To burn or not to burn? Refuse problem up to city. Way is being sought to make all city's waste useful again. (Los Angeles municipal news. v. 1, no. 3 (May 1, 1912), p. 1, 3.)

Loughborough, England.

1896

Butterworth, Arthur Shaw. Loughborough sewage and refuse disposal works. (Minutes of Proceedings Institution of Civil Engineers. v. 125, p. 367-376.) **VDA**

Louisville, Ky.
See also below, Rochester, N. Y. under date of 1906.
Annual report of the department of street cleaning. 1894 (1st published)-1911. (In: Annual reports of the city, 1894-1911.)
* **SYA**
Biennial compilation of the ordinances of Louisville, 1-4, 7-9. 1895-1901, 1907-1911.
* **SYA**
Contain the ordinances relative to garbage removal, removal of dead animals and relative to the street cleaning deparment.

Lowell, Mass.
Serial
Annual report of the Board of Health, 1878-1911. (In: Annual reports of the city, 1878-1911.) * **SYA**

Includes reports of removal of garbage and ashes. Since 1891 Lowell has operated a refuse cremator under the control of the health board.
Annual report of the superintendent of streets, 1876-1911. (In: Annual reports of the city, 1876-1911.) * **SYA**
Non-serial

1907

Disposal of garbage at Lowell, Mass. 250 w. (Municipal journal and engineer. v. 22, p. 503.) †† **SER**

Lübeck, Germany.
Strassenreinigung, 1892, 1899/1900-1909-/10. (In: Lübeck. Jahresberichte der Verwaltungsbehörden, 1892, 1899/1900-1909-/10.) * **SYD**

Lüneburg, Germany.

1902

Kampf. Die Abfuhranstalt der Stadt Lüneburg. (Zeitschrift für Architectur und Ingenieurwesen. 1902, p. 399-418.) **MQA**

Luxembourg.

1903

Müllabfuhr und Strassenreinigung in Luxembourg. (Zeitschrift für Transportwesen und Strassenbau. Jahrg. 22, p. 263-264.) †† **TPB**

Lyons, France.
See also above the General Works, under date of 1884.

1908

Enlèvement des immondices à Lyon. (La Technique sanitaire. Année 3 (suppl.), p. 6.) **SPA**

McKeesport, Pa.

1908

Garbage disposal at McKeesport [Pa.]. 600 w., 2 drawings, 1 illus. (Municipal journal and engineer. v. 25, p. 390.) †† **SER**

Magdeburg, Germany.
Strassenreinigungswesen, 1899/1900-1909-/10. (In: Magdeburg. Bericht über die Verwaltung, 1899/1900-1909/10.) * **SYD**

Manchester, England.
See also above the General Works, under dates of 1888 and 1898.
Particulars of expenditures and statement of work done by the cleansing department, 1890/1-1910/11. (In: Manchester. Council proceedings, 1890/1-1910/11.)
* **SYB**

Mannheim, Germany.
See also above the General Works, under date of 1907.
Abfuhrwesen, 1900-1902. (In: Mannheim. Chronik der Hauptstadt Mannheim. Jahrg. 1-3, 1900-1902.) * **SYD**

Mansfield, O.

1899

Report on sewage and garbage disposal for Mansfield. (Ohio. Board of Health. 15. annual report 1899/1900, p. 138-148.) **SPB**

Special Cities — Mansfield, cont'd.

SNOW and BARBOUR, Boston, Mass. Report to Mayor Brown of Mansfield, O. on refuse disposal in towns. (Municipal engineering. v. 17, p. 99-100.)   **VDA**

Marburg, Germany.

1900

ORTSSTATUT betreffend die Uebernahme der Abfuhr des Strassenkehrichts, einschliesslich Schnee und Eis, sowie der Hausabfälle. (Deutsche Vierteljahrsschrift für öffentliche Gesundheitspflege. v. 33, p. 620-622.)   **SPA**
Text of the principal paragraphs, viz. 1-4. The ordinance was adopted at the time the city undertöok the matter of refuse disposal.

Marion, O.

1899

REPORT on sewage and garbage disposal for Marion. (Ohio. Board of Health. 15. annual report. 1899/1900, p. 149-158.)   **SPB**

1906

PIERSON, George H. Sewage purification and refuse incineration plant, Marion, O. (Engineering record. v. 53, p. 358-362.)   †† **VDA**

PRATT, R. Winthrop. Combined septic tanks, contact beds, intermittent filters and garbage crematory, Marion, O. (Engineering news. v. 55, p. 197-201.)   †† **VDA**

VEREINIGTE Abwasserreinigungs- und Müllverbrennungsanlage in Marion, Ohio. (Zeitschrift für Transportwesen und Strassenbau. Jahrg. 23, p. 243-246; illus.)   †† **TPB**

Marquette, Mich.

1911

TEXT of ordinance for the collection and disposal of garbage and refuse; July 17, amended Oct. 2. (United States. Public Health and Marine Hospital Service. Public health reports. v. 27, p. 806.)   **SPB**

Marseilles, France.
See also above the General Works, under date of 1884.

1910

DISPOSAL of refuse from the streets in Marseilles. 970 w. (United States. Monthly consular and trade reports. March 1910 (no. 354), p. 169.)   **TLG**

Milan, Italy.

1903

FERRI, Luigi. Pulizia stradale urbana ed igiene. (Giornale della Reale Società Italiana d'Igiene. v. 25, p. 467-470.)   **SPA**

Milwaukee, Wis.
See also above the General Works, under dates of 1894 and 1909.

Serial

ANNUAL report of the superintendent of garbage collection, 1908-1911. (In: Milwaukee. Health Board. Annual report, 1908-1911.)   **SPB**

Non-serial

1889

MARTIN, R. Disposal of garbage at Milwaukee. (Amer. Public Health Association. Public health papers and reports. v. 15, p. 63-64.)   **SPA**
Brief description of the Merz reduction system. Dr. Martin was commissioner of health of Milwaukee at the time.

1893

WINGATE, U. O. B. The collection and disposition of animal and vegetable waste in the city of Milwaukee. (American Public Health Assoc. Public health papers and reports. v. 19, p. 48-52.)   **SPA**
Dr. Wingate was commissioner of health of Milwaukee at the time.

1902

GARBAGE collection, removal and final disposal at Milwaukee. 5000 w., 1 foldg. pl. (Engineering news. v. 47, p. 63-64.)
History of garbage disposal at Milwaukee with description of new Engle incinerating furnaces.

GARBAGE cremation plant at Milwaukee, Wis. 1 pl. (Supplement to Engineering news. Jan. 23, 1902.)   †† **VDA**

INCINÉRATION des ordures ménagères à Milwaukee. (Le génie civil. v. 40, p. 280-281; illus.)   †† **VA**

1908

GARBAGE disposal in Milwaukee. 2,800 w. (Engineering record. v. 57, p. 107.)   †† **VDA**
Review of report by Rudolph Hering recommending a 300-ton incinerating plant.

GARBAGE and refuse disposal. 1200 w. (Engineering record. v. 57, p. 2.)   †† **VDA**
Editorial comment on plan for garbage disposal at Milwaukee and Columbus, O.

HERING, Rudolph. Report accompanied by plans and specifications for a refuse incinerator in Milwaukee. (Milwaukee. Proceedings of the Common Council. 1908/9, p. 59-60.)   * **SYA**
The report only is printed in the proceedings.

MILWAUKEE refuse disposal report. 1,800 w. (Municipal journal and engineer. v. 24, p. 189.)   †† **SER**
Review of report by Rudolph Hering recommending a 300-ton incineration plant, with utilization of heat.

REPORT on garbage and refuse disposal, Milwaukee, Wis. 3,500 w. (Engineering news. v. 59, p. 54.)   †† **VDA**
Review of report by Rudolph Hering recommending for Milwaukee a combined garbage destructor and electrical plant.

SPECIFICATIONS and bids for an incinerating and power generating plant for Milwaukee. 4500 w. (Engineering news. April 22, 1909.)   †† **VDA**
Comment on the specifications.

SPECIFICATIONS for the erection and completion of a refuse incinerator. Oct. 1908. (Milwaukee. Proceedings of the Common Council. 1908/9, p. 727-745.)   * **SYA**
The text is full of the specifications.

1909

GREELEY, Samuel A. Refuse disposal and the new refuse incineration plant for Milwaukee. (Journal Assoc. of Engineering Societies. Boston, v. 43, p. 171-184.)   **VDA**

Special Cities — Milan, cont'd.

1910

GREELEY, Samuel A. The construction and testing of the Milwaukee refuse incinerator. 7000 w., illus. (Engineering news. v. 64, p. 60.)   †† VDA
Mr. Greeley is superintendent of the incinerator.

HERING, Rudolph. Modern practice in the disposal of refuse. 3500 w. (Journal American Public Health Assoc. v. 1, p. 910.)   SPA

—— Same. (Engineering record. Sept. 24, 1910.)   †† VDA
Remarks on the Milwaukee incinerator and a discussion of the best methods now in use for the disposal of city refuse.

MILWAUKEE garbage destructor. (Power and the engineer. v. 32, p. 2097-2099; illus.)   †† VFA

MILWAUKEE incinerating plant. 2000 w. (Municipal journal and engineer. June 29, 1910.)   †† SER
Method of testing this plant.

SLY, Fred S. Refuse disposal in Milwaukee. illus. (Municipal journal and engineer. v. 28, p. 643-650.)   †† SER

TESTS of the Milwaukee refuse destructor. 3000 w. (Engineering record. July 16, 1910.)   †† VDA

1911

FOSTER, Pell W. Disposal of city wastes. ⌐Description of a 300-ton Heenan Destructor for the city of Milwaukee.⌐ (School of Mines quarterly. New York University. v. 32, p. 149-155.)   OA

MILWAUKEE refuse incinerator. (Municipal engineering. v. 41, p. 148.)   VDA

1912

METHODS of garbage collection in Milwaukee, present and proposed. 4000 w. (Engineering and contracting. March 20, 1912.)   †† VDA

Minneapolis, Minn.
See also above the General Works, under date of 1910.

Serial

ANNUAL report of the inspector of the crematory 1902 (1st)-1910. (In: Minneapolis. Annual report of the health board, 1902-1910.)   *SYA

Non-serial

1888

PROPOSED garbage cremation in Minneapolis. 400 w. (Engineering and building record. v. 18, p. 122.)   †† VDA
Descriptive article from the Minneapolis "Pioneer-press" with editorial comment.

1901

DECARIE, The, garbage crematory at Minneapolis. (Engineering record. v. 44, p. 318-319.)   †† VDA

1906

See below Rochester, N. Y., this date.

1910

GARBAGE collection and disposal in Minneapolis, Minn. (Municipal engineering. v. 39, p. 275-276; 2 illus.)   VDA

TEXT of rules for garbage and ash collection. (Municipal journal and engineer. v. 28, p. 120.)   †† SER

1911

HALL, P. M. Garbage collection. (Municipal journal and engineer. v. 30, p. 120.)   †† SER
Relates to garbage receptacles only. Paper read before the American Public Health Association.

Miskolcz, Hungary.
See above the General Works under date of 1908.

Molenbeek-St. Jean, Belgium.
⌐TRAITEMENT des immondices à Molenbeek-St. Jean.⌐ (La Technique sanitaire. Année 4 (suppl.), p. 90-91.)   † SPA

Moline, Ill.

1900

KITTILSEN, Edward. Garbage collection and disposal at Moline, Ill. (Engineering news. v. 43, p. 90.)   †† VDA

Montclair, N. J.

1911

GARBAGE disposal in Montclair, N. J. (Municipal engineering. v. 41, p. 147.)   VDA

Montgomery, Ala.

1912

PRIMROSE, John. A 60-ton refuse destructor at Montgomery, Ala. 800 w.; illus. (Engineering news. June 20, 1912.)   †† VDA

Montreal, Canada.

1887

LABERGE, L. The destruction of garbage. (American Public Health Assoc. Public health papers and reports. v. 13, p. 233-241.)   SPA
Review of experience at Montreal in the incineration of waste, and description of the Mann incinerator.

1894

THACKERAY garbage incinerator for the city of Montreal. 1,500 w., 1 folding pl. (Engineering news. v. 32, p. 451.)   †† VDA
First plant in America to utilize heat of incineration. Direct feeding from garbage carts and rapid drying of garbage are improvements claimed.

1899

NOTES on the operation of the Montreal garbage furnace. 1,100 w. (Engineering news. v. 42, p. 374.)   †† VDA
Thackeray incinerator is used, built along English lines. Waste is burned without sorting and with no additional fuel.

1902

PELLETIER, Elzear. Refuse disposal in Montreal. (American Public Health Assoc. Public health papers and reports. v. 28, p. 29-45.)   SPA
A report submitted to the board of health of the Province of Quebec.

1906

See below Rochester, N. Y., this date.

Special Cities, cont'd.

Moss Side, England.
See also above the General Works under date of 1903.

1904
See above Brussels, this date.

Muncie, Ind.

1905
SANITARY garbage incinerator. 1100 w., 1 illus. (Municipal engineering. v. 29, p. 224.) **VDA**
Tests of a Decarie incinerator at Muncie, Ind.

Munich, Germany.
See also above the General Works, under dates of 1884 and 1899.

Serial
REINLICHKEITSPOLIZEI. Bericht, 1882/7-1911. (In: Munich. Bericht der Gemeindeverwaltung, 1882/7-1911.) ***SYD**
On house refuse collection and disposal and street cleaning. This material is particularly useful, both historically and economically. The report for 1899 contains a detailed cumulative table from 1891, the year following a reorganization of the system of refuse collection. Another cumulative table covering 1898-1902 appears in the report for 1902.

STATISTISCHER Monatsbericht der Stadt München, 1898-1912. **†SDG**
Caption 43, each month, gives statistical returns relating to domestic refuse removal.

Non-serial
1899
TEXT of police regulation of Jan. 22, 1898, for the care and removal of house refuse. (Zeitschrift für Transportwesen und Strassenbau. v. 16, p. 579-580.) **TPB**

1901
WEYL, Th. Die Sortieranstalt der Müllverwertung München G. m. b. H. zu Puchheim. (Fortschritte der Strassenhygiene. Heft 1, p. 51-58; illus.) **†VDH**

1905
MÜLLVERARBEITUNG in München. (Zeitschrift für Transportwesen und Strassenbau. Jahrg. 22, p. 77.) **††TPB**

Nashville, Tenn.

1911
MUNICIPAL, A, garbage incinerator and steam generator. (Municipal engineering. v. 41, p. 405-406.) **VDA**
Under construction at Nashville, Tenn.

Nelson, England.
See above the General Works under dates of 1901 and 1904.

Serial
ANNUAL report of the garbage contractor, 1898-1910. (In: New Bedford. Annual report of the health board, 1898-1910.) ***SYA**

Non-serial
1897
SPECIFICATIONS for the collection and disposal of garbage. (In: New Bedford. Annual report of the health board. 1897, p. 4-6.) ***SYA**

1906
GARBAGE reduction [in New Bedford, Mass.] (Municipal engineering. v. 31, p. 414-415.) **VDA**

1908
GARBAGE disposal at New Bedford [Mass.] 1,600 w., 2 illus. (Municipal journal and engineer. v. 24, p. 233.) **††SER**
Description of reduction plant and its operation.

New Orleans, La.

1879
THOMPSON, Hugh Miller. Method introduced by the Auxiliary Sanitary Association for disposing of the garbage of New Orleans. (American Public Health Assoc Public health papers and reports. v. 5, p. 32-34.) **SPA**
With a plate showing dump carts and garbage scow in use in New Orleans.

1896
See above, Cincinnati, this date.

1909
GARBAGE collection and disposal plans for New Orleans. (Municipal engineering. v. 37, p. 49-50.) **VDA**

New York City.
See also above the General Works under date of 1906.

Serial
1 series
ANNUAL report of the Board of metropolitan police commissioners, 1-13. 1857-1869. **SLY**
Contains material on street cleaning and garbage removal. This board was abolished by the Act of April 5, 1870, creating the Police Department.

2 series
Under Act of April 5, 1870.
ANNUAL report of the police department, 1-3. 1870/1-1872/3. **SLY**
No annual reports of this board were published after that for 1872/3. Quarterly reports, however, were printed for these years in the City record, references to which are on file in room 229.

3 series
(Coleman Administration)
Under Laws of 1881, chap. 367.
REPORT of the department of street cleaning, 1886-1887/8. **VDHA**
No other annual reports were made. Each report reviews the work of the department from its origin in 1881. James S. Coleman was commissioner.

REPORT for the quarter ending March 31, 1883 [to the quarter ending Dec. 31, 1894]. (In: New York City. City record. v. 11-23.) ***SYA**
Exact references are on file in room 229.

4 series
(Waring Administration)
Under chap. 269, Laws of 1892 "An Act to amend sections 45, 704, 705, 707, 708, 710 and 1936 of chap. 410, Laws of 1882, entitled 'An act to consolidate into one act and to declare the special and local laws affecting public interests in the city of New York,' so as to secure the more efficient cleaning of the streets, avenues, public places, wharves, piers and heads of slips in said city."
The passage of this Act and the consequent reorganization of the street cleaning department were the outcome of the report of the special committee appointed by Mayor Grant (see below the Non-serial

Special Cities — New York, cont'd.

group under date of 1891). The first and only commissioner to be appointed under this act was George E. Waring, jr. who took office on Jan. 15, 1895, and served for three years, or until a change in the organization of the department was effected by the Greater New York charter of 1897.

Col. Waring made no annual reports. He did make one comprehensive report covering the term of his administration, and which is entered below among the Non-serials under date of 1898.

REPORT for the quarter ending March 31, 1895 ιto the quarter ending Dec. 31, 1897ι. (In: New York City. City record. v. 23-26.) **SYA**

Exact references are on file in room 229.

5 series

Under the Greater New York charter of 1897. Commissioners: 1898–1899, James McCartney; 1899–1902, Percy E. Nagle; 1902–1906, M. Craven; 1906–1909, Foster Crowell; William H. Edwards, 1909–date.

REPORT of the department of street cleaning for the year ending Dec. 31, 1898-1910. **VDHA**

No report was issued for 1901. The reports for 1902–1905 are in one volume, published in 1906. The report for 1910 the Library has only as it was printed in the City record for Sept. 1911, p. 7667–7670. The report for 1911 has not yet been printed. The report of Commissioner McCartney for 1898 is abstracted to the extent of 1100 words, in the Engineering record. v. 40, p. 30 et seq.   ††VDA

Non-serial

1695-1701

ιNOTE on street cleaning systems in vogue.ι (New York City. Common Council. Manual 1862, p. 525.)   **SAM**

1778

PROCLAMATION by Major General James Robertson, commandant of New York, providing for cleansing the streets and for the removal of waste; March 23. (New York City. Common Council. Manual. 1863, p. 658.)   **SYA**

1806

ιNOTE on method of street sweeping in vogue.ι (New York City. Common Council. Manual. 1857, p. 421.)   **SAM**

1845

COMMUNICATION from the comptroller in relation to unexpended balance for cleaning streets. n. t.-p. (New York City. Board of Aldermen. Documents. 1845, p. 69-72. doc. 6.)   **SYA**

1850

COMMUNICATION to the Mayor from Prof. Hare in relation to removal of dead animal substances etc. from streets. n. t.-p. p. 1259-1266. 8°. (New York City. Board of Aldermen. Documents. 1850, no. 80.)   **SYA**

LAWS relating to carts and cartmen, public porters and handcartmen. New York: Bowne and Co., 1850. 32 p. 24°.

1851

ORDINANCE, An, for licensing and otherwise regulating the use and employment of carts and cartmen, dirt carts and dirt cartmen, etc. New York: Bowne & Co., 1851. 29 p. 8°.   **VDH p.box 1**

1854

COMMUNICATION from the chief of police in answer to a resolution directing him to report why laws and ordinances in relation to throwing garbage and ashes into the streets are not enforced. n. t.-p. p. 247-256. 8°. (New York City. Board of Aldermen. Documents. 1854, no. 12.)   **SYA**

COMMUNICATION of the commissioner of streets and lamps with copy of contract for cleaning streets. Jan. 20. n. t.-p. 24 p. 8°. (New York City. Board of Aldermen. Documents. 1859, no. 26.)   **SYA**

COMMUNICATION of the comptroller in relation to the contract with W. B. Reynolds for removal of dead animals, offal, etc., transmitting the testimony taken before the recorder. n. t.-p. p. 757-850. 8°. (New York City. Board of Aldermen. Documents. 1854, no. 43.)   **SYA**

COMMUNICATION from the comptroller in reply to a resolution relating to cleaning streets. n. t.-p. p. 347-362. 8°. (New York City. Board of Aldermen. Documents. 1854, no. 18.)   **SYA**

REPORT of the public health committee in favor of concurring with the Board of Councilmen in resolution to pay W. B. Reynolds amount due him on contract for removal of blood, offal and other refuse substances from the city. n. t.-p. p. 575-612. 8°. (New York City. Board of Aldermen. Documents. 1854, no. 38.) **SYA**

SPECIFICATION for cleaning streets in the city of New York. n. t.-p. 11 p. 8°.   **VDHA p.box**

1855

PROPOSITION for the removal of dead animals, offal, etc., free of expense to the city. n. t.-p. 6 p. 8°. (New York City. Board of Aldermen. Documents. 1855, no. 27.)   **SYA**

REPORT of the committee on street cleaning recommending that no action be taken on the communication from the commissioner of streets and lamps in regard to street cleaning machines. n. t.-p. 4 p. 8°. (New York City. Board of Aldermen. Documents. 1855, no. 18.)   **SYA**

REPORT of the special committee on removal of offal, etc. n. t.-p. 42 p. 8°. (New York City. Board of Aldermen. Documents. 1855, no. 41.)   **SYA**

1856

REPORT of the street cleaning committee in relation to amending sec. 6 of the specifications for advertising for cleaning the streets of the city, together with a minority report on the same subject. n. t.-p. 8°. (New York City. Board of Aldermen. Documents. 1856, no. 30.)   **SYA**

COMMUNICATION from the commissioner of the office of streets and lamps with a detailed statement of expenditures of the street cleaning bureau from Jan. 1 – March 22, 1856. n. t.-p. 12 p. 8°. (New York City. Board of Aldermen. Documents. 1856, no. 20.)   **SYA**

Special Cities — New York, cont'd.

1857

[Note on method of street sweeping and garbage removal in vogue. (New York City. Common Council. Manual. 1857, p. 434.) **•SAM**

Report of the city inspector in reference to cleaning the streets from May 1 to Aug. 1, 1857. n. t.-p. 20 p. 8°. (New York City. Board of Aldermen. Documents. 1857, no. 19.) **•SYA**

Report of the special committee on streets appointed by the Councilmen to inquire into the cause of the present filthy condition of the streets. New York, 1857. 1 p.l., 172 p. 8°. **VDHA**

1865

Report of the council of hygiene and public health of the Citizens' Association of New York upon the sanitary condition of the city. New York: D. Appleton and Co., 1865. cxliii, 360 p. 8°. **SPB**
Garbage removal is only incidentally treated of, but there is sufficient material to make the volume of use to one considering the subject historically.

1866

Contracts for the cleaning of the streets and for the removal of offal and night soil from the cities of New York and Brooklyn. New York, 1866. 20 p. 8°. **VDHA p.box**

1874

New York Common Pleas. General Term. Charles Devlin, plaintiff respondent against the Mayor. Case and exceptions. Appeal from judgment. Hackley street cleaning contract. New York, 1874. 1736 p. 4 v. 8°. **VDH**

Report of the Committee on the Affairs of Cities of New York State relative to the management of the Street Cleaning Bureau of the Police Board. 888, 6 p. 8°. (New York State. Assembly documents. 1874, no. 122, v. 8.) **•SBK**

1878

New York Municipal Society. Report of a committee appointed by the Society to draft a bill providing for cleaning the streets. 18 p. 8°. **VDHA p.box**

New York Municipal Society. Report of a committee appointed by the Society to investigate the system of street cleaning, as administered by the Board of police in the City of New York, read before the Society, Jan. 7, 1878. 54 p. 8°. **SER p.v.2**
—— A second copy. **VDHA p.box**

188–

Circular letter from the commissioner of the street cleaning department to occupants of houses relative to removal of snow from sidewalks. broadside. 4°. **†† VDG p.v.3, no.14**

1880

Chandler, C. F. Plan for a bureau of street cleaning. 11 p. 4°. **VDHA p.box**

Circular from the Committee on affairs of cities of New York State relating to the improvement of the street cleaning in New York City. Feb. 16, 1880. 2 l. 4°. **†† VDK p.v.1, no.51**

Report of the Committee on Affairs of Cities, of New York State, on street cleaning in New York, and means for a more efficient method. Albany, 1880. 59 p. (New York State. Assembly documents. 1880, no. 112. v. 8.) **•SBK**

1881

Opinion of the medical profession on the condition and needs of the city of New York, in regard to street cleaning; expressed in a mass meeting of the physicians of the city, held April 13, 1881. New York, 1881. 32 p. 8°. **VDH p.box 1**

Report of the citizens' committee of twenty-one on efforts to reform the system of cleaning streets. New York: D. Taylor, 1881. 40 p. 8°. **VDH p.box**

Special laws, ordinances of the Board of Aldermen and rules and regulations of the Board of Health and Department of Police affecting the Department of Street Cleaning. New York, 1881. 52 p. 8°. **VDHA p.box**

1884

Estimate [blank] for the cleaning of the streets, for the removal of snow and ice therefrom, and for the collection of ashes, garbage and street sweepings, and the removal of the same in the first street-cleaning district. 1884. 4 f. 4°.
—— Same, second street-cleaning district. 1884. 4 f. 4°.

Proposals for estimates for the cleaning of the streets, for the removal of snow and ice therefrom, and for the collection of ashes, garbage, and street sweepings, and the removal of the same in the first street-cleaning district. 1884. 17 f. 4°.
—— Same, second street-cleaning district. 1884. 20 f. 4°.

1885

Methods of street cleaning and garbage removal in New York. 1500 w. (Sanitary engineer. v. 11, p. 541.) **VDA**

1886

Proposals for estimates for cleaning the streets, for removal of snow, etc. in first street cleaning district. 21 f., 1 plan. f°. **VDK p.v.1, no.9**
—— Same; second street cleaning district. 21 f. f°. **VDK p.v.1, no.10**

1887

New York Ladies' Health Protective Association. Memorial to Abram S. Hewitt on the subject of street cleaning. 12 p 8°. **VDH p.box 1**

1890

Contract no. [ ] for cleaning the streets, removal of snow, etc. in the first street-cleaning district. 20 f. f°. **†† VDK p.v.1, no.7**

Special Cities — New York, cont'd.
—— Same, second street-cleaning district. 21 f. f°.   †† **VDK p.v.1, no.6**
CONTRACT no. [ ] for the final disposition of the ashes, garbage and street sweepings. 21 f. f°.   †† **VDK p.v.1, no.8**

1891

EXAMINATION, An, of the subject of street cleaning in the City of New York made by the street cleaning committee at the request of Hon. Hugh J. Grant, Mayor. New York, 1891. 153 p., 1 map. 8°.   **VDHA**
—— Same, a second copy.   **IR p.box**
The committee was composed of Morris K. Jesup, Charles F. Chandler, Francis V. Greene, Thatcher M. Adams and D. H. King, jr.

1893

COMMUNICATIONS addressed to the Mayor by the Street Cleaning Department relative to the requirements of the Department. 4 f.   †† **VDK p.v.1, no.14**
REPORT of Commissioner Andrews of the Street Cleaning Department to His Honor the Mayor. Sept. 15, 1893. 13 p. 8°.
      VDHA
With recommendations for the more efficient management of the department.
STREET cleaning bill proposed by the Citizens committee of New York. 1893. 14 f. f°.   †† **VDK p.v.1, no.11**

1894

See also above London, England, this date.
PUMPELLY, Josiah Collins. Clean streets. 7 p. (Municipal program leaflet no. 2.)
      VDH p.box 1
REPORT of the advisory committee appointed by Mayor Gilroy to investigate the manner of garbage disposal best suited for New York. (Engineering record. v. 31, p. 2-3.)   †† **VDA**
See also editorial on p. 1.
The committee was composed of Franklin Edson, Thomas L. James, Daniel Delehanty, Charles G. Wilson, and W. S. Andrews.
—— Same, condensed. 1000 w. (Engineering news. v. 32, p. 452.)   †† **VDA**
—— Same, reviewed. (Zeitschrift für Transportwesen und Strassenbau. Jahrg. 12, p. 3-4.)   †† **TPB**
MORSE, William F. The collection and disposal of refuse of large cities. (American Public Health Assoc. Journal. v. 20, p. 187-195.)   **SPA**
Presents briefly the plan laid before the advisory board appointed by Mayor Gilroy on the "Final Disposition of the Refuse of N. Y. C."
WARING, George E., jr. The disposal of a city's waste. (North American review. v. 161, p. 49-56.)   *DA
New York City; division of waste and uses it can be put to.

1896

AGNEW, S. H. Street cleaning in New York. (City government. v. 1, p. 1-3.)
      †† **SER**
FORM of estimate and contract for the final disposition of garbage. 24 p. 4°.
      †† **VDK p.v.1, no.2**
HITCH your wagon to a star. (Garden and forest. v. 9, p. 251-252.)   **VQA**
Editorial; general remarks on Col. Waring's work.

MERZ Universal Extractor and Construction Co. Facts concerning the disposal of garbage in New York City. 18 p. 8°.
      VDI p.box 5
WARING, George E. Report on final disposition of wastes. 159 p. 8°. (New York City. Street Cleaning Department.)
      VDIA p.box
—— Same, reviewed by E. Vallin. (Revue d'hygiène et de police sanitaire. v. 19, p. 64-67.)   **SPA**
—— Same, review. (Engineering news. v. 35, p. 118-119.)   †† **VDA**
—— Same, abstract. 2000 w. (Engineering record. v. 34, p. 124.)   †† **VDA**

1897

LETTER of the West End Association to the Mayor on the removal of ashes, etc. 29 p. 8°.   **VDI p.box 1**
LIVACHE, Achille. Procédés de traitement des ordures ménagères à Philadelphie et à New York, leur application au traitement des ordures ménagères de la ville de Paris. (Bulletin de la Société d'encouragement pour l'industrie nationale. v. 96, part 1, p. 172-190.)   **VDA**
—— Same, condensed. 4500 w., 3 drawings, 3 illus. (Le Génie civil. v. 31, p. 89.)   †† **VA**
MUNTZ, Achille. Rapport présenté au nom du comité d'agriculture, sur un travail de M. Livache intitulé Procédés de traitement des ordures ménagères, etc. (Bulletin de la Société d'encouragement pour l'industrie nationale. v. 96, part 1, p. 169-172.)   **VDA**
STREET cleaning in New York; a successful labor experiment. (Gunton's magazine. v. 13, p. 172-181.)   **TAA**
An abstract of Col. Waring's report made April 5, 1897.
WARING, George E., jr. The cleaning of a great city. (McClure's magazine. v. 9, p. 911-924; illus.)   *DA
History of his reorganization of the Street Cleaning Department, New York City.

1898

LABOR, The, question in the Department of Street Cleaning. Being an account of the first year's work of the Committee of 41 and the Board of Conference. New York: M. B. Brown, 1897. 14 p. 8°.
A report made by Col. Waring to Mayor Strong on April 5, 1897.
LETTER to the presidents of Juvenile Leagues of the Department of Street Cleaning. 3 p. 8°.
STREET cleaning in New York. (Independent. v. 49, p. 105-106.)   *DA
WARING, George E., jr. Report by George E. Waring, jr., of the Department of Street Cleaning for 1895-96-97. I. Observations on street cleaning methods in European cities. II. Review of the general work of the Department. III. Report of the snow inspector. IV. The adjustment of labor questions by the "Committee of 41" and the "Board of Conference." New York, 1898. 1 p.l., 234 p., 1 pl., 5 tables. 8°.
      VDHA

Special Cities — New York, cont'd.

—— Same. (In: Municipal affairs. v. 2, no. 2, supplement.)   **SERA**
Part I of the report contains Col. Waring's observations made in the summer of 1896 on the methods of street cleaning employed by the cities of Vienna, Budapest, Munich, Berlin, Cologne, Brussels, London, Birmingham, Paris, Turin and Genoa. Part II, covering p. 79–193 contains reports of the master mechanic, of the chief of the bureau of final disposition, special reports on waste disposal (i. e. The private collection of garbage; The traffic in waste paper; The fuel value of city ashes) and on factors in the cost of street sprinkling. Part III relates to snow removal. Part IV relates to the labor question in the Street Cleaning Department.

1899

CITY Waste Disposal Co. organized from the staff of the late Col. G. E. Waring, jr. Consulting and contracting in sewage disposal, garbage and refuse disposal and street cleaning. 14 p. 12°.   **VDIA p.box**
GIBSON, F. M. Street cleaning in New York. (Public improvements. v. 1, p. 4-5.)   **† SER**
GONDEN, H. J. Garbage and other city wastes. (Public improvements. v. 1, p. 273-277.)   **† SER**
WALKER, John Brisben. Great problems in organization. V. The street-cleaning work of Colonel Waring in New York. (Cosmopolitan. v. 26, p. 234-235.)   *** DA**
Brief summary of Col. Waring's work and methods.

1900

ABOUT cremating New York's garbage. (City government. v. 8, p. 1-2.)   **†† SER**
BAKER, E. Burgoyne. Refuse of a great city. (Munsey. v. 23, p. 81-90.)   *** DA**
DOTY, Alvah H. Report on disposition of garbage. 197 p. 8°. (New York State. Assembly Documents. 1900, no. 67. v. 15.)   *** SBK**
MEADE, Charles A. City cleansing in New York; some advances and retreats. (Municipal affairs. v. 4, p. 721-741.)   **SERA**

1901

MORSE, William F. Street Cleaning Department under Tammany. New York, 1901. 37 p.   **VDHA p.box**
Reprinted from the New York vigilant.
WEYL, Th. Die Verwertung des Küchenmülls on New York. (Fortschritte der Strassenhygiene. Heft 1, p. 67-74; illus.)   **† VDH**

1902

GARBAGE, The, destructor at Bellevue Hospital. (Engineering review. v. 12, p. 4-5.)   **†† VEA**
HAMLIN, A. D. F. Our public untidiness. (Forum. v. 33, p. 322-332.)
HOUSE-REFUSE incinerator for New York City. 1,400 w., 7 drawings. (Engineering record. v. 45, p. 372.)   **†† VDA**
Separate incinerator to be installed for light, readily combustible refuse.
NOTICE to householders, tenants, etc. issued by the Department of Street Cleaning, relative to the cleaning of streets and sidewalks and removing the snow and dirt therefrom. 2 l. 8°.   **VDG p.v.3**
Text in English, German, Italian and Hebrew.

PROPOSED light refuse crematory for New York City. 1,700 w., 12 drawings. (Engineering news. v. 47, p. 314.)   **†† VDA**
REED, W. B. Removal of snow and ice in the Borough of Manhattan. (Street railway journal. v. 12, p. 839-840.)
SOPER, George A. Report on the disposal of the refuse of New York City. (American Public Health Assoc. Public health papers and reports. v. 28, p. 64-74.)   **SPA**
Good historical summary of the various authorities directing the street cleaning of New York City.

1903

DISPOSAL of New York's refuse. (Scientific American. v. 89, p. 292-294.)   **†† VA**
ORDINANCE, An, regulating the cleaning of streets and sidewalks... Also the sanitary code and the tenement house act as to garbage and ash receptacles. 5(1) p. folder. narrow 8°.
WOODBURY, John McGraw. Wastes of a great city. (Scribner's magazine. v. 34, p. 387-400.)   *** DA**

1904

BATTEY, Arthur H. New York's snow problem. (Municipal journal. v. 16, p. 54-56.)   **†† SER**

1906

ANALYSIS by the Bureau of municipal investigation and statistics of the Finance Department of the departmental estimate for 1907 for the Bureau of Street Cleaning. 25 p. 4°.   **VDHA**
BUREAU of Municipal Research, New York. Some phases of the work of the Department of street cleaning of New York City. Prepared by the Bureau of City Betterment of the Citizens' Union. New York, 1906. 2 p.l., 48 p. 8°.   **VDH p.v.1, no.7**
REPORT of the Street cleaning department committee of the Board of Aldermen on the administration of the department of street cleaning. Adopted by the Board of Aldermen, July 10, 1906. 132 p. 8°.   **VDH**
The "Ivins report."
—— Same. (In: New York City. Proceedings of the Board of Aldermen. 1906, v. 2, 1089-1227.)   *** SYA**
STEARNS, Fred L. General information about the Department of street cleaning. New York, 1906. 113 p., illus. 8°.   **VDHA**

1907

BERNHEIMER, C. S. The Street cleaning department and the East Side. (Charities. v. 18, p. 450-451.)   **SHK**
CHISOLM, B. O. Street cleaning difficulties in New York. (Same. v. 18, p. 590-594.)   **SHK**
FETHERSTON, J. T. Street cleaning accounts... system employed by the Bureau of street cleaning, borough of Richmond; great reduction in cost of work effected thereby. (Municipal journal and engineer. v. 23, p. 3-10.)   **†† SER**

Special Cities — New York, cont'd.
1908
FETHERSTON, J. T. Municipal refuse disposal. (Proceedings American Soc. of Civil Engineers. v. 34, p. 345-442.)   **VDA**
MORSE, William F. The collection and disposal of municipal waste. New York: Municipal journal and engineer [cop. 1908]. xii, 462 p. illus. 8°.   **VDI**
Deals largely with methods in New York City.
MORSE-BOULGER Destructor Co. Sanitary disposal of waste. 48 p. 8°. **VDI p.box 4**
PARSONS, H. de B. City refuse and its disposal. 2500 w.; illus. (Scientific American supplement. July 4, 1908.) †† **VA**
Disposal of New York City refuse.
REPORT of the commission on street cleaning and waste disposal appointed by Mayor McClellan on June 11, 1907. (City record. v. 36, p. 1162-1202.)   *** SYA**
The commission was composed of H. de B. Parsons, Rudolph Hering and Samuel Whinery.
—— Same, condensed. (Zeitschrift für Transportwesen und Strassenbau. Jahrg. 25, p. 209-211.)   †† **TPB**
—— Same, extracts and general review. 7500 w. (Engineering news. v. 59, p. 449.)   †† **VDA**
See also editorial, p. 462.
—— Same, review. 3300 w. (Engineering record. v. 57, p. 207.)   †† **VDA**
RUBBISH incineration in New York. 1,500 w., 8 illus. (Municipal journal and engineer. v. 24, p. 466.)   †† **SER**
History and developments. See also editorial, p. 467.
VERY, Edward D. Collection and final disposition of city wastes by the N. Y. Department of Street Cleaning. (Journal of the Society of Chemical Industry. v. 27, p. 379.)   **VOA**
1909
RUBBISH and snow removal. (Municipal journal and engineer. v. 27, p. 919-922.)   †† **SER**
An illustrated account of methods in use in New York City, with extracts from an address by Wm. H. Edwards, the commissioner of street cleaning.
STREET flushing in New York. (Municipal journal and engineer. v. 27, p. 960-961; illus.)   †† **SER**
Includes a table of data of street cleaning tests.
1910
MORSE, William F. Disposal of the city's waste. (American city. v. 2, p. 119-122; 177-180.)   **SERA**
NEW YORK street cleaning. Two thousand miles of streets covered; amount of rubbish, ashes and garbage collected; organization of forces; collection and disposal; methods of measuring snow; juvenile league. 5000 w.; illus. (Municipal journal and engineer. v. 29, p. 45.)   †† **SER**
REAL estate owned by the City of New York under the jurisdiction of the Department of street cleaning, boroughs of Manhattan, the Bronx and Brooklyn. Jan. 1, 1910. 34 p. illus. 4°.   **VDH**
Published by the New York City Finance Department.
VERY, E. D. Tests of street flushing or washing machines, Department of Street

Cleaning, New York City. 1500 w. (Engineering news. April 14, 1910.) †† **VDA**
1912
[NEWSPAPER clippings of May and September, 1912.]   **Room 229**
RULES and regulations for the transportation of refuse material from the City of New York; adopted at a meeting of the board of health on April 9, 1912. (City record. April 16, 1912. p. 3187-3188.)   *** SYA**

BARREN ISLAND
Serial
ANNUAL report on inspection of the rendering plant at Barren Is., 1898-1909. (In: New York State. Annual report of board of health, 18-30. 1898-1909.) **SPB**

Non-serial
1897
UTILIZATION of New York city garbage. 1,600 w., 1 drawing, 6 illus. (Scientific American, v. 77, p. 97, 102.)   †† **VA**
Description of Barren Island plant.
1898
LANDRETH, Olin H. Barren Island garbage disposal plant. 1,500 w. (Engineering record, v. 38, p. 275.)   †† **VDA**
Report to New York state board of health describing operations of this plant. Garbage is cooked with steam under pressure and the liquid separated in presses. Grease is recovered from the liquid. Some objectional odors are given off.
1899
REFUSE disposal at Barren Island, New York. 2,000 w. (Engineering record, v. 39, p. 208.)   †† **VDA**
Abstract of report by committee to investigate offensiveness of reduction processes for the disposal and utilization of dead garbage of New York City.
1900
BARREN Island garbage reduction works, greater New York. 7,700 w., 1 drawing, 6 illus., 1 map., 1 folding pl. (Engineering news, v. 43, p. 66.)   †† **VDA**
Detailed description of this large plant. Arnold system of reduction is used.
DISPOSAL of city wastes and the Barren Island garbage reduction works. 4,000 w. (Engineering news. v. 43, p. 76.)   †† **VDA**
History of the plant. Advises cautious consideration before abolition of the plant as proposed.
1908
VERY, Edward D. Collection and final disposition of city wastes by the New York department of street cleaning. 1,600 w. (Journal of the Society of Chemical Industry. v. 27, p. 380.)   **VOA**
Contains brief description of reduction plant at Barren Island.
1911
VALUE of New York's garbage; method of treating it at Barren Island; amounts treated; sums received by company from the city and from salable products. 1500 w. (Municipal journal and engineer. v. 30, p. 611.)   †† **SER**

Special Cities — New York, cont'd.

DELANCEY SLIP

1905

EDMANDS, S. S. Electric light from rubbish in New York city. 3,000 w., 4 drawings. (Engineer, Chicago. v. 42, p. 577.) †† **VDA**
Description of combined rubbish incinerator and electric-lighting plant at Delancey slip, Manhattan. Light rubbish only is burned.

1906

PARSONS, H. de B. Disposal of municipal refuse, and rubbish incineration. 38 p., 4 diagr., 4 drawings, 9 illus., 3 folding pl. (Transactions of the American Society of Civil Engineers. v. 57, p. 45.) **VDA**
Consideration of the composition of refuse, and its fuel value. Description of incinerating plant at Delancey slip, New York.

FORTY-SEVENTH STREET

PROPOSED crematory for street sweepings and light refuse, New York City. (Engineering news. v. 53, p. 228; illus.) **VDA**
—— Same. (Zeitschrift für Transportwesen und Strassenbau. Jahrg. 22, p. 243-244; illus.)   †† **TPB**

GOVERNOR'S ISLAND

See also above the General Works, under dates of 1894 and 1905, resp.

1885

REILLY, H. I. A garbage-cremator at Governor's Island. 350 w., 1 drawing. (Sanitary engineer. v. 12, p. 211.) **VDA**
Successful results obtained by drying garbage on grate, then using dry garbage as fuel.

STANTON STREET

1901

RUBBISH incineration in New York and the design for the new Stanton Street incinerator. (Engineering record. v. 49, p. 128-131.) †† **VDA**

NEW BRIGHTON

See also above the General Works, under date of 1908.

Serial

ANNUAL report of the bureau of street cleaning. 1902-1909. (In: Annual report of the President of the Borough of Richmond, 1902-1909.) *****SYA**
These reports are all made by J. T. Fetherston, the superintendent, and they are particularly complete as regards refuse collection and disposal.

Non-serial

1897

GARBAGE-DISPOSAL system of New Brighton, 900 w. (Engineering record. v. 35, p. 319.) †† **VDA**
Brownlee cremator.

1906

FETHERSTON, J. T. Report to the President of the Borough of Richmond. Examinations of refuse destructors in England, Ireland, Scotland, Wales, and Canada, made May to August 1906. [New York: M. B. Brown,] 1906. 44 p., 15 pl., 5 tables. 8°. (N. Y. City. Street Cleaning Dept.) **VDH**

REFUSE disposal in the borough of Richmond, New York. 1,600 w., 5 drawings. (Engineering record. v. 54, p. 628.) †† **VDA**
Discusses plans for destructors of the British type and the guarantees required.

REFUSE disposal for Staten Island. 2,600 w., 5 drawings. (Municipal journal and engineer. v. 21, p. 558.) †† **SER**
Plans and specifications for refuse destructor plant, with utilization of heat for steam generation. See also editorial, p. 587.

SPECIFICATIONS for refuse destructor, borough of Richmond, New York City. 2,500 w., 2 drawings. (Engineering news. v. 56, p. 592.) †† **VDA**
See also editorial, p. 595.

1907

GEPLANTE Anlage für Hausmüllverbrennung für den Stadtbezirk Richmond in New York. (Zeitschrift für Transportwesen und Strassenbau. Jahrg. 24, p. 43-44.) †† **TPB**

REFUSE destruction for the borough of Richmond, New York City. 2,200 w. (Municipal engineering. v. 32, p. 39.) **VDA**

1908

NEW refuse destructor at West New Brighton, N. Y. 2,500 w., drawings, 5 illus. (Engineering record. v. 58, p. 386.) †† **VDA**
Heenan and Froude destructor, in which mixed refuse (ashes, garbage and refuse) is burned.

NEW refuse destructor for West New Brighton, borough of Richmond, New York City. 2,800 w., 2 drawings, 2 illus. (Engineering news. v. 60, p. 485.) †† **VDA**

REFUSE destruction in Richmond borough, New York City. 2,500 w. (Municipal engineering. v. 35, p. 359.) **VDA**
Extracts from report by J. T. Fetherston. See also editorial, p. 376.

RICHMOND borough refuse destructor. 3,200 w., 3 diagr., 2 drawings, 5 illus. (Municipal journal and engineer. v. 25, p. 447.) †† **SER**
Review of report by J. T. Fetherston, superintendent of street cleaning, borough of Richmond, New York City.

RIKER'S ISLAND

RIKER'S Island refuse conveyor plant. 1500 w., 2 drawings, 2 illus. (Engineering record. v. 50, p. 335.) †† **VDA**

WILLIAMSBURG BRIDGE

1905

BURR, S. D. V. New York rubbish incinerating plant utilized to light Williamsburg Bridge. (Iron age. v. 77, p. 496-499; illus.) † **VDA**

COMBINED rubbish destructor and power plant in New York. 4,000 w., 9 drawings, 2 illus. (Engineering record. v. 52, p. 537.) †† **VDA**
Plant located beneath the Williamsburgh Bridge.

1906

ANLAGE für Verbrennung von leichtem Hausmüll und Strassenkehricht in New York. (Zeitschrift für Transportwesen und Strassenbau. Jahrg. 23, p. 6-9; illus.) †† **TPB**

Special Cities — New York, cont'd.

INCINERATOR and lighting plant. 400 w. (Municipal journal and engineer. v. 21, p. 629.) †† SER
Record of tests of plant for lighting the Williamsburgh Bridge, New York City.

Newark, N. J.

1902

BIDS for garbage collection and disposal, Newark, N. J. (Municipal engineering. v. 23, p. 116-117.) **VDA**

1903

GARBAGE collection ordinance [synopsis]. (Municipal engineering. v. 24, p. 54.) **VDA**

1906

See below Rochester, N. Y., this date.

Newcastle-upon-Tyne, England.

LAWS, W. George. Refuse burning. (Transactions 7th International Congress of Hygiene and Demography. v. 7, p. 210-218.) **SPA**
Relates largely to Newcastle-upon-Tyne.

Newport Naval Training Station.

See also above, the General Works, under date of 1909.

1909

BAKENHUS, R. E. The garbage crematory of the Newport Naval Training Station. 2500 w., illus. (Engineering record. v. 59, p. 218-220.) †† **VDA**
FOUR à incinérer les gadoues de Newport [i. e. U. S. Naval Training Station]. (Le Génie civil. v. 55, p. 117, illus.) †† **VA**

Newton, Mass.

1895

REPORT of the Board of Health upon sanitary disposition of garbage and other municipal waste and the reorganization of the department. [Newton] 1895. 19 p. 8°.

Nottingham, England.

See also above, the General Works, under date of 1904.

1908

GARBAGE and refuse as fuel in Nottingham, England. (Municipal engineering. v. 35, p. 394.) **VDA**

Norristown, Penn.

1888

WEAVER, J. K. Disposal of garbage in Norristown. (Pennsylvania. Board of Health. Annual report. 6, 1888/9, p. 462-467.) **SPB**

Oak Park, Ill.

See also above, the General Works under date of 1909.

1908

A 40-ton garbage incinerator at Oak Park, Illinois. illus. (Engineering record. v. 58, p. 408-409.) †† **VDA**
Describes a plant for a suburban town of about 20,000 population. Domestic garbage only is collected.

Oil City, Penn.

1911

TEXT of regulations of the board of health for the collection and disposal of garbage and refuse; Oct. 18. (United States. Public Health and Marine Hospital Service. Public health reports. v. 27, p. 966.) **SPB**

Oldham, England.

See also above, the General Works under date of 1898, 1899 and 1904.

Omaha, Nebr.

See also above, the General Works, under date of 1911.

The annual report of the city engineer of Omaha for 1899 contains comparative statistics on street cleaning in 40 American cities. The matter is reproduced in Municipal engineering. v. 18, p. 200-201. **VDA**

Orange, N. J.

1911

TEXT of ordinance regulating disposal of refuse; Dec. 1. (United States. Public Health and Marine Hospital Serice. Public health reports. v. 27, p. 522.) **SPB**

Padua, Italy.

1908

PELLEGRINI, F. Contributo sperimentale allo studio del contenuto batterico della polvere stradale, con speciale riguardo alle vie di Padova. Verona, 1908. 32 p. 8°.
Reviewed in Revue d'hygiène et de police sanitaire. v. 31, p. 1146-1147. **SPA**
Dissertazione di laurea (Contribution expérimentale a l'étude de la teneur bactérienne de la poussière des rues, avec considérations speciales à la voirie de Padoue, thèse de doctorat). Entrepris à l'Institut d'hygiène de l'Université de Padoue.

Paisley, Scotland.

See also above, the General Works, under dates of 1902 and 1903, resp.

1903

ECONOMICS of refuse destruction. (County and municipal record. v. 1, p. 373-374.) **SPA**
Relates to Paisley; table showing cost of cleansing previous to installation of 8-cell Horsfall destructor in 1901 and cost since.

1905

PAISLEY refuse destructor. Installation of electric light. (County and municipal record. v. 4, p. 324-325.) **SPA**

Panama Canal Zone.

1910

GARBAGE disposal. Method of collection and disposal in Canal Zone, Panama and Colon. (Canal record. v. 4, p. 11.) † **TSB**
—— Same. (Engineering-Contracting. Sept. 28, 1910, p. 273.) **VDA**

Paris, France.

See also above, the General Works, under date of 1886, 1894 and 1899 resp.

1842

BAYARD, Henri. Mémoire sur la topographie médicale du IV° arrondissement de la ville de Paris. Recherches historiques et statistiques sur les conditions hygié-

Special Cities — Paris, cont'd.

niques des quartiers qui composent cet arrondissement. (Annales d'hygiène publique. ser. 1, v. 28, p. 1-46; 241-309.) **SPA**
p. 20–25, 289–293 relate to street hygiene from the time of Philippe-Auguste to the revolution.

1843

TEXT in French of the police ordinance of April 1, 1843, prescribing garbage removal and street cleaning for Paris. (Annales d'hygiène publique. ser. 1, v. 40, p. 461-467.) **SPA**
This ordinance was in effect a sanitary code and was regarded at the time a model not only for the larger French but by foreign cities as well.

1849

NEIGES et glaces. (Annales d'hygiène publique. ser. 1, v. 44, p. 457-459.) **SPA**
Text of the ordinance of Dec. 31, 1849, for the removal of ice and snow from the streets of Paris.

CHEVALLIER, A. Notice historique sur le nettoiement de la ville de Paris depuis 1184 a l'époque actuelle. (Same. ser. 1, v. 42, p. 262-319.) **SPA**

1877

VAISSIÈRE. Notice sur le nettoiement de la voie publique à Paris. (Annales des ponts et chaussées. Mémoires et documents. ser. 5, v. 13, p. 66-118.) **VDA**

VAUTHIER. Rapport présenté au nom de la 3ᵉ commission du conseil municipal relatifs aux depenses du service de la voie publique dans Paris. (Annales industrielles. 1877, p. 536-539; 598-606.) **††VA**

— Same, reviewed. (Minutes of Proceedings of the Institution of Civil Engineers. v. 52, p. 375-376.) **VDA**

1882

DU MESNIL, O. Des dèpots de voiries de la ville de Paris, considerées au point de vue de la salubrité. (Revue d'hygiène et de police sanitaire. v. 4, p. 37-57; 101.) **SPA**
Historical summary of legislative provisions.

1883

COMMISSION Technique de l'Assainement de Paris.
The report of the commission itself is not, at this time, in the Library. A synopsis of the findings and the text of the regulations adopted by the commission are printed in Le Génie civil. v. 3, p 597-599. **††VA**
These regulations constituted a code for the guidance of the municipal engineers.

1885

See also above London, England, this date.
COMMISSION Supérieur de l'assainissement de Paris. 4° sous-commission. Étude de diverses questions relatives à l'hygiène. 4° sous-commission spéciale. Procédés à employer pour l'enlèvement et l'utilisation des ordures ménagères. Séances du 13 février ä 21 mai, 1885. 100 p. 4°. **†SPC**

DU MESNIL, O. Transport par chemins de fer des matières infectes gadoues, suifs, os, sang, cuirs verts, etc.): projet de reglementation. (France. Recueil des travaux du comité consultatif d'hygiène publique de France. v. 15, p. 213-223.) **SPC**

— Same, résumé. 15 p. 4°. (Commission supérieur de l'assainissement de Paris. 4° sous-commission. 4° sous-commission speciale.) **†SPC**

— De l'enlèvement et du transport des immondices et des ordures ménagères. (Annales d'hygiène publique. ser. 3, v. 16, p. 179-188.) **SPA**
Relates largely to methods in vogue in Paris, but is based on official reports received from Lille, Lyon, Bordeaux, Marseille, Havre, Bruxelles, Amsterdam, London, Glasgow, Rome, Berlin, Vienna, Dresden, Munich, St. Petersburgh and Moscow.

— La viabilité de Paris. Étudiée au point de vue de l'hygiène. (Annales d'hygiène publique. ser. 3, v. 17, p. 247-274.) **SPA**
p. 263–274 relate to street cleaning and waste removal. There are tables showing quantity of waste removed each year 1865–1884 and cost of removal.

1892

BASSINET, A. Rapport présenté au nom de la 3ᵉ commission sur le projet d'ètablissement de gares d'embarquement, pour les ordures ménagères, aux lignes de l'Est, de l'Ouest, du Nord et d'Orléans. 7 p. 4°. (Paris. Conseil Municipal. Rapports et documents. 1892, no. 115.) **∗SYC**

1893

DU MESNIL, O. Les ordures ménagères de Paris. Eloignement et utilisation agricole. (Annales d'hygiène publique. ser. 3, v. 29, p. 549-555.) **SPA**

1894

SEYRIG, William. Procédè nouveau de traitement des ordures ménagères. 1,200 w., 3 drawings. (Le Génie civil. v. 24, p. 414.) **††VA**
Reduction process, proposed for Paris, which would leave a final product suitable for fertilizer.

1895

BONVILLAIN. Traitement industriel et utilisation des ordures ménagères. (Revue d'hygiène et de police sanitaire. v. 17, p. 912-914.) **SPA**
Paper read before the Congrès de l'assainissement, Paris, 1895. Relates largely to Paris.

VITOUX, Georges. ⌐Destructor furnace erected at the Quai de Javel, Paris. (La Revue technique. Sept. 1895, p. 385.)

— Same, reviewed. (Minutes of Proceedings of the Institution of Civil Engineers. v. 123, p. 498-499.) **VDA**
The original is not, at this time, in the Library.

1896

BROUARDEL and DU MESNIL. Immondices: transport par chemins de fer; destruction par le feu. (France. Recueil des travaux du comité consultatif d'hygiène publique de France. v. 26, p. 173-247.) **SPC**
The second part "Incinération des ordures ménagères," p. 191 et seq., contain reports on the systems obtaining in Paris, Berlin and Brussels.

PETSCHE. Essai à Paris de destruction par le feu des ordures ménagères. (Le Génie civil. juin 1896, p. 9.)
The original is not, at this time, in the Library.

— Same, reviewed. (Revue d'hygiène et de police sanitaire. v. 18, p. 755-757.) **SPA**

1897

See above New York City, this date.

Special Cities — Paris, cont'd.

1898

See also above Brussels, this date.

BRET, E. Balayeuse-arroseuse automobile de la ville de Paris. illus., 1 pl. (Génie civil. v. 52, p. 425-429, 457-459.) †† VA

LE BRETON. Rapport présenté au nom de la 3ᵉ commission sur l'enlèvement des ordures ménagères de la ville de Paris. 126 p. 4°. (Paris. Conseil municipal. Rapports et documents. 1898, no. 102.)
*SYC

1899

BILLET, Emma. Street cleaning in Paris. (Public improvements. v. 1, p. 58-59 and 63.) † SER

LE BRETON. Rapport au nom de la 3ᵉ commission sur le renouvellement des marchés pour l'enlèvement des ordures ménagères. 51 p. 4°. (Paris. Conseil Municipal. Rapports et documents. 1899, no. 10.) *SYA
See also no. 75 in the same volume.

1900

BERANECK, Hermann. Die Stadt Paris vom gesundheitstechnischen Standpunkte. (Zeitschrift für Transportwesen und Strassenbau. v. 17, p. 217-220, 232-234.) †† VA
Relates chiefly to the sewerage system, although street cleaning and refuse removal are touched upon.

VINCEY, P. Les ordures ménagères de Paris. (Mémoires de la Société des Ingénieurs Civils de France. Année 1900, v. 1, p. 643-647.) VDA
—— Same, reviewed. (Minutes of Proceedings of Institution of Civil Engineers. v. 143, p. 377-378.) VDA
—— Same, reviewed. (Annales d'hygiène publique. ser. 3, v. 45, p. 278.) SPA

NOTICE monographique sur les ordures ménagères de Paris. 129 p., 1 diagr., 4 illus., 2 maps. (Bulletin de la Société d'Encouragement pour l'Industrie Nationale. v. 100, p. 172, 510, 816.) VDA
Detailed discussion of collection, transportation and disposal of garbage of Paris for agricultural purposes.

1902

BRET, E. L'arrosement de la voie publique à Paris. (Le Génie civil. v. 40, p. 275-280; illus.) †† VA
—— Same, reviewed. (Municipal engineering. v. 23, p. 40-41.) VDA

1905

SPRENGWAGEN mit Dampfbetrieb für die Stadt Paris. (Zeitschrift für Transportwesen und Strassenbau. Jahrg. 22, p. 283-285, 304-306, illus.) †† TPB

1906

CHANGE in garbage disposal methods at Paris from grinding and utilization to incineration. 900 w. (Engineering news. v. 56, p. 252.) †† VDA

1908

AUTOMOBIL-SPRENGWAGEN und Strassenkehrmaschine der Stadt Paris. (Zeitschrift für Transportwesen und Strassenbau. Jahrg. 25, p. 361-362, 377-380, 401-403; illus.) †† TPB

BERGES, P. Aristide. L'évacuation et l'utilisation des ordures ménagères. 3500 w. (Génie civil. Sept. 26, 1908.) †† VA
Suggests an improved method of dealing with garbage disposal problem of Paris.

1910

CHERIOU, Adolphe. Rapport au nom de la 3ᵉ commission sur la réorganisation du service de nettoiement et sur une nouvelle répartition des sections et circonscriptions du service de la voie publique. 67 p., 2 maps. 4°. (Paris. Conseil Municipal. Rapports et documents. 1910, v. 3, no. 133.) *SYC
p. 29-48 are given over to a consideration of house refuse removal with a résumé of systems in vogue in other cities.

GARBAGE disposal in Paris. (Municipal engineering. v. 39, p. 224.) VDA

GIROU, Georges. Rapport au nom de la 3ᵉ commission sur la réorganisation des usines de traitement des ordures ménagères et l'organisation nouvelle de l'ensemble du service. 7 p. 4°. (Paris. Conseil Municipal. Rapports et documents. 1910, no. 39.) *SYC

MASON, Frank H. Garbage disposal in Paris. 520 w. (U. S. Monthly consular and trade reports. June, 1910, no. 357, p. 111.) TLG

1911

BLANCHARD, Raphael. Les immondices de Paris. (Revue d'hygiène et de police sanitaire. v. 33, p. 997-999.) SPA
Review by F. H. Renaut of the original article in Gazette des hôpitaux; 1911, p. 251, 269.

1912

LABORDÈRE, P. L'évacuation des ordures ménagères à Paris. Automobiles pour collecte et le transport aux usines. (Le Génie civil. v. 60, p. 461-464; illus.) †† VA
Description of the large automobile trucks with 6 cubic meter capacity used by the street cleaning department of Paris, and their efficiency.

Partick, Scotland.
See also above the General Works, under dates of 1902 and 1904.

1902

BRITISH refuse lighting plant. 2000 w., 2 drawings, 3 illus. (Electrical world. v. 39, p. 725.) †† VGA
Destructor at Partick.

PARTICK electricity and refuse destructor works. (Municipal record and sanitary journal. v. 1, p. 29-31.) SPA

PARTICK municipal electricity and destructor works. 2,300 w., 2 drawings, 4 illus., 1 map. (Electrician, London, v. 48, p. 892.) †† VGA

NEW destructor and electric lighting installation at Partick. (Sanitary journal. v. 8, p. 676-677.) SPA

Paterson, N. J.

1911

BIDS for garbage plant at Paterson, N. J. (Municipal engineering. v. 41, p. 483.) VDA

Special Cities, cont'd.

Pavia, Italy.

1900

FERRARIS, Ernesto. L'immondezza stradale nella città di Pavia dal punto di vista dell'igiene pubblica. (Giornale della Reale Società Italiana d'Igiene. v. 22, p. 97-121.)
SPA

Pforzheim, Germany.
See also above, the General Works under date of 1909.

1907

HERZBERGER and MORAVE. Projekt einer Müllverbrennungsanstalt mit Klärschlammtrocknungsanlage für die Stadt Pforzheim. (Gesundheits-Ingenieur. Jarhg. 30, p. 649-656.)   **††SPA**

Philadelphia, Pa.

Serial

1 series

ANNUAL report of the department of highways, 1882-1886. (In: Philadelphia. Mayor's message with accompanying documents, 1882-1886.)   ***SYA**
Contain reports on street cleaning. Prior to 1882 the work of street cleaning was done under the supervision of the board of health. The reports of this board contain no material on the subject. The report of the department of highways for 1882 contains a table of expenditures for ash and garbage removal and for street cleaning for each year from 1877 to 1881.

2 series

ANNUAL report of the bureau of street cleaning, 1-22. 1887-1909. (In: Philadelphia. Annual report of the board of public works, 1887-1909.)   ***SYA**

Non-serial

1884

[BLANK form for] Proposal for collecting and removing kitchen garbage and offal for the year 1884. [Specifications for collecting and removing kitchen garbage and offal for the year 1884.] n. t.-p. 21. f°. (Philadelphia. Highway Department.)

1893

DOWLING garbage cremator. 500 w. (Engineering record. v. 29, p. 77.)   **††VDA**
Cremator in use in Philadelphia.

1897

See above New York City, this date.

1898

CIVIC Club of Philadelphia. Leaflet for the officers of the League of good citizenship. Some of the city regulations for street cleaning and the removal of ashes, garbage and rubbish. [Philadelphia, 1898.] 2 l. 16°.

Pittsburgh, Pa.

1888

PITTSBURGH garbage cremator. 250 w. (Engineering and building record. v. 18, p. 276.)   **††VDA**
Letter from Rider Garbage Furnace Co. giving results of a year's operation.

1895

GARBAGE collection and disposal at Pittsburgh, Pa. 2,800 w., 1 illus. (Engineering news. v. 34, p. 218.)   **††VDA**
Reduction process used. System of collection considered at some length.

1900

GARBAGE reduction works at Pittsburgh and Allegheny, Pa. 3,000 w. (Engineering news. v. 43, p. 214.)   **††VDA**
Operation of plant of American Reduction Co., with history. See also editorial, p. 208.

1911

PITTSBURGH, The, garbage problem. (Municipal engineering. v. 41, p. 61-62.) **VDA**
Synopsis of a report made by Director Walters of the Health Department.

Plumstead, England.
See above, the General Works, under date of 1904.

Plymouth, England.

1910

PATON, James. The collection and disposal of house refuse in Plymouth. [With discussion.] (Journal Royal Sanitary Institute. v. 31, p. 155-163.)   **SPA**

Pomona, Calif.

1911

TEXT of ordinance no. 352 for the collection, removal and disposal of garbage; Sept. 5. (United States. Public Health and Marine Hospital Service. Public health reports. v. 27, p. 967.)   **SPB**

Port Glasgow, Scotland.

1904

NEW, The, destructor at Port-Glasgow (County and municipal record. v. 3, p. 34-36.)
Meldrum simplex; two cuts showing interior and exterior views resp. are given.

Port Ontario, N. Y.
See also above, the General Works, under date of 1909.

1907

AN 18-ton garbage crematory. 800 w., 2 drawings, 1 illus. (Engineering record. v. 55, p. 462.)   **††VDA**

Portland, Ore.

Serial

ANNUAL report of the garbage crematory, 1904-1908. (In: Portland. Mayor's message and municipal reports, 1904-1908.)   ***SYA**

ANNUAL report of the street cleaning department, 1903-1908. (In: Portland. Mayor's message and municipal reports, 1903-1908.)   ***SYA**

Non-serial

1896

HAWKS, A. McL. Garbage crematory at Portland, Ore. 800 w., 2 drawings. (Engineering news. v. 36, p. 125.)   **††VDA**
Consists of a combustion furnace and a "gas-consuming" furnace. Forced draft is supplied to roasting-oven by small blowing-engine.

Special Cities — Portland, cont'd.

1908

See below, Seattle, this date.

Prague, Bohemia.

1908

PINKUSZ. Müllbeseitigung in Prag. (Gesundheits-Ingenieur. Jahrg. 31, p. 171.) †† **SPA**
Abstract of a paper in Oesterreichische Wochenschrift für den öffentlichen Baudienst.

Prahran, Victoria.

1906

BRITISH dust destructors in Australia. ti. e. Prahran.} (Sanitary record. v. 38, p. 403.) † **SPA**

1908

REFUSE destructor at Prahran, Victoria. 800 w., 3 illus. (Municipal journal and engineer. v. 24, p. 397.) **VDA**
Meldrum destructor.

REPORT of the chief clerk of the Adelaide board of health on a personal inspection of the Prahran destructor. (Adelaide. Notice, Papers, etc. of the City Council. 1907-/8, p. 204-205.) * **SYB**

1910

CALDER, William. Municipal waste ₍Prahran₎.' 4500 w. (Surveyor. v. 37, p. 21-23.) †† **VDA**

Providence, R. I.

Serial

ANNUAL report of the superintendent of health, 1-29. 1883-1911. **SPB**
Contain reports on garbage and ashes removal.

Non-serial

1866

REPORT upon the removal of swill and house offal, and other subjects. Presented to the Board of Health June 25th, 1866, by the superintendent of health. Providence: Providence Press Co., 1866. 13 p. pap. 8°. (Providence, R. I. Health Board. City document 1866-67. no. 4.) * **SYA**

1892

CHAPIN, Charles V. The disposal of garbage in the city of Providence, R. I. (American Public Health Assoc. Public health papers and reports. v. 18, p. 258-264.) **SPA**

1902

CHAPIN, Charles V. The collection and disposal of garbage in Providence, R. I. (American Public Health Assoc. Public health papers and reports. v. 28, p. 46-50.) **SPA**

1911

ARONOVICI, Carol. Municipal street cleaning. A survey of the problem of street cleaning in the city of Providence. Providence, 1911. 34 p. 8°.
Part 1 of the annual report for 1911 of the Rhode Island Industrial Statistics Bureau for 1911.

Reading, Pa.

1907

GARBAGE problem at Reading. 650 w. (Municipal journal and engineer. v. 22, p. 200.) **VDA**

Rhondda, Wales.

1902

REFUSE disposal in the Rhondda. (Sanitary record. v. 30, p. 78.) † **SPA**

Richmond, England.

1884

BEEHIVE refuse destructor. 1300 w. (Building news and engineering journal. v. 47, p. 402.) **MQA**
-— Same. (Engineering news. v. 14, p. 133.) †† **VDA**
Describes destructor of this type in operation in Richmond, England.

Richmond, Va.

Serial

ANNUAL report of the superintendent of street cleaning, 1902 (1st)-1911. (In: Richmond. Annual reports of the city, 1902-1911.) * **SYA**

Rochdale, England.
See also above, the General Works, under dates of 1898 and 1904.

1895

BROOKMAN, F. W. Power from town refuse. (Cassier's magazine. v. 9, p. 569-575; illus.). **VDA**
Working of Meldrum destructor at Rochdale, Eng.

Rochester, N. Y.
See also above, the General Works, under dates of 1907 and 1908.

1894

REPORT of special committee relative to site for garbage reduction plant. (In: Rochester. Proceedings of the Common Council. 1894, p. 379.) * **SYA**

1900

SLOCUM and DENTON. Communication to the Common Council in relation to the Hogel garbage contract. (In: Rochester. Proceedings of the Common Council. 1900, p. 22-24.) * **SYA**

1906

FISHER, Edwin A. Report on the collection and disposal of garbage and other city refuse in the city of Rochester, N. Y. Also description of plants and methods in other cities. Rochester, 1906. 61 p., 1 l. 8°.
Includes reports of personal inspections of the Cleveland and Buffalo plants, and extracts, etc. on operations in Buffalo, Newark, Boston, Grand Rapids, Minneapolis, Detroit, Columbus, Lexington, New York City, St. Louis, Louisville, Washington, D. C. and Montreal.

1907

MAYOR's message relative to site for garbage reduction plant. (In: Rochester. Proceedings of the Common Council. 1907, p. 80.) * **SYA**

Special Cities, cont'd.

Rome, Italy.
See above, the General Works, under the date of 1884.

St. Albans, England.

1908

E$_{LE}$C$_{TR}$I$_{CITY}$ supply at St. Albans; a combined refuse destructor and generating plant. 3000 w., 3 illus., 5 drawings. (Electrical engineering, London.   v. 4, p. 805.)
†† **VGA**

St. Cloud, France.

1892

DU MESNIL, O. Rapport sur l'installation d'un dèpot d'immondices à Saint-Cloud. (Revue d'hygiène et de police sanitaire. v. 14, p. 53-55.)   **SPA**

St. Helens, England.

1900

HIGHFIELD, J. S. Destructor and electric power station at St. Helen's. 900 w. (Electrical review, London. v. 47, p. 7.) †† **VGA**

St. Louis, Mo.
See also above, the General Works, under the dates of 1894, 1906 and 1911.

Serial

ANNUAL report of the general foreman of garbage and dead animals removal, 1904-/5-1909/10. (In: St. Louis. Annual report of the board of public improvements, 1904/5-1909/10.)   ***SYA**

ANNUAL report of the street cleaning and scavenger department, 1872/3-1873/4. (In: St. Louis. Mayor's message and accompanying documents, 1872/3-1873/4.) ***SYA**
Continued as:

ANNUAL report of the street commissioner, 1877/8-1909/10. (In: Same, 1877/8-1909/10.)   ***SYA**

Non-serial

1903

CHARLES, Benjamin H. Garbage destruction for St. Louis. (Municipal engineering. v. 25, p. 257-258.)   **VDA**

1905

SYSTEMS of garbage collection and disposal. (Municipal engineering. v. 28, p. 393-395.)   **VDA**
Extracts from report of health commissioner Simon of St. Louis.

1906

See also above, Rochester, this date.
GARBAGE collection and disposal in St. Louis. (Municipal engineering. v. 30, p. 214-221.)   **VDA**
Extracts from report of the Sanitation Committee of the Civic League of St. Louis and a report by Howard G. Bayles, of New York, prepared under instructions from A. J. O'Reilly, president of the board of public improvements of St. Louis.
GARBAGE disposal in St. Louis. 1,200 w. (Municipal journal and engineer. v. 20, p. 241.)   †† **SER**
Brief review of report by the public sanitation committee of the Civic Improvement League of St. Louis, recommending disposal by reduction.

GARBAGE incineration for St. Louis. 1,500 w. (Municipal engineering. v. 30, p. 28.)
VDA
Extracts from report by Joseph G. Branch.

1907

GARBAGE disposal at St. Louis. 1,100 w. (Municipal journal and engineer. v. 23, p. 372.)   †† **SER**
Conditions are given under which bids for disposal by reduction will be received. See also article, p. 553.

1908

McCULLOUGH, J. F. St. Louis garbage disposal. 1,600 w. (Bulletin of the League of American Municipalities. v. 9, p. 84.)
†† **SER**
Gives specifications for garbage reduction bids of various firms.

1909

CASEY, Charles C. Garbage collection and disposal in St. Louis. (Municipal journal and engineer. v. 27, p. 553-557; illus.)   †† **SER**
NEW, The, garbage reduction plant at St. Louis. (Engineering record. v. 60, p. 13-16; illus.)   †† **VDA**

1910

ST. LOUIS garbage reduction plant. 800 w. (Municipal journal and engineer. v. 28, p. 620.)   †† **SER**
Initial inadequacy of plant to handle garbage and remedy.

1911

SUGGESTED garbage receptacle ordinance drafted by the Civic League of St. Louis. (Municipal engineering. v. 40, p. 445.)
VDA

St. Ouen, France.

1906

DELAHAYE, Ph. De la conversion des ordures ménagères de Paris en engrais complets aux usines de Saint-Ouen, Issy et Romainville. (La Technique sanitaire. Année 1, (suppl.), p. 88-89.)   † **SPA**

St. Paul, Minn.
See also the Council proceedings of St. Paul for much material of an administrative nature relating to garbage.

Serial

ANNUAL report of the superintendent of garbage collection, 1900-1910. (In: St. Paul. Annual report of the health board, 1900-1910.)   **SPB**

Non-serial

1888

HOYT, Henry F. Proposed plan for the disposition of nightsoil, garbage, &c., at St. Paul, Minn. (American Public Health Assoc. Public health papers and reports. v. 14, p. 40.)   **SPA**

1889

REPORT of the special committee on disposition of refuse matters. (St. Paul. Proceedings of the Common Council. 1889, p. 131-132.)   ***SYA**
The committee investigated conditions in the cities of Chicago, Milwaukee and Buffalo.

Special Cities — St. Paul, cont'd.

1892

HOYT, Henry F. The collection, removal and disposal of garbage and dead animals at St. Paul. 1,300 w. (American Public Health Assoc. Public health papers and reports. v. 18, p. 115.)   * SPA

1911

TEXT of ordinance regulating disposal of refuse; July 14. (United States. Public Health and Marine Hospital Service. Public health reports. v. 27, p. 200.)   SPB

Salt Lake City, Utah.
See above, the General Works, under date of 1911.

Saltley, England.

1904

ROBERTS, D. J. Description of refuse destructor and electrical power generating station in course of erection at Saltley. 3,800 w., 4 drawings. (Electrical engineer, London. v. 40, p. 384.)   †† VGA

San Francisco, Cal.

Serial

ANNUAL report of the bureau of streets, 1901/2-1903/4. (In: San Francisco. Annual report of the public improvements board, 1901/2-1903/4.)   * SYA

Continued as:

ANNUAL report of the street cleaning department, 1904/5-1909/10. (In: Same, 1904-/5-1909/10.)   * SYA
The 1903/4 report has a special report on street cleaning in Los Angeles.

ANNUAL report of the garbage inspector, 1910. (In: San Francisco. Annual report of the health board, 1909/10.)   * SYA
The position was created on March 1, 1910.

Non-serial

1898

How San Francisco disposes of its garbage. 2,000 w., 7 illus. (Scientific American. v. 79, p. 260.)   †† VA
Thackeray incinerator in successful operation for eight months.

STREET cleaning in San Francisco. (Municipal engineering. v. 17, p. 98.)   VDA

1900

MILLS, F. J. Thackeray garbage furnaces at San Francisco, Cal. 4,700 w., 3 drawings, 3 illus. (Engineering news. v. 43, p. 318.)   †† VDA
Garbage is burned, with no additional fuel and with few objectionable features.

1901

See above Indianapolis, this date.

1908

See below, Seattle, this date.

1910

GARBAGE incinerators for San Francisco. Study of composition of refuse, methods of sampling and testing, average amounts per month, relative amount of ashes, garbage and rubbish, etc. 4500 w.; illus. (Municipal journal and engineer. v. 29, p. 325.)   †† SER

SPECIFICATIONS for determining cost of garbage incineration. 3500 w.; illus. (Engineering and contracting. v. 34, p. 171-172.)   † VDA
Specifications issued by the San Francisco board of public works relative to tests and cost.

Scranton, Pa.
See also above, the General Works, under date of 1911.

1888

GARBAGE cremator proposed for Scranton. 200 w. (Engineering and building record. v. 18, p. 270.)   †† VDA
Description of proposed Engle cremator.

1893

VIVARTTAS system of garbage disposal, Scranton, Pa. 450 w., 1 drawing. (Engineering record. v. 28, p. 265.)   †† VDA
Gases of combustion utilized steam used in preliminary drying. Coal is used only in starting the cremator.

1909

GARBAGE incineration in Scranton. 2200 w. (Municipal journal and engineer. v. 26, p. 159-162.)   †† SER

Seattle, Wash.
See also above, the General Works, under date of 1909.

1905

See below, Tacoma, this date.

1908

GARBAGE disposal in the Northwest. 800 w. (Municipal journal and engineer. v. 25, p. 746.)   †† SER
Review of the report of a San Francisco committee after investigation of incinerating plants at Seattle, Portland, Ore., and Vancouver.

MORSE, William F. Seattle refuse destructor. 1,500 w., 3 illus. (Municipal journal and engineer. v. 24, p. 520.)   †† SER
Meldrum type, the first destructor of English design to be erected in United States.

NEUE, Die, Müllverbrennungsanlage in Seattle. (Zeitschrift für Transportwesen und Strassenbau. Jahrg. 25, p. 422-424.)   †† TPB

OPERATING results of the Seattle refuse destructor. 400 w. (Engineering record. v. 58, p. 440.)   †† VDA
Results from three months' operation of a Meldrum destructor.

SIXTY-TON refuse destructor in Seattle, Washington. 3,000 w., 6 drawings, 2 illus. (Engineering record, v. 57, p. 583.)   †† VDA
Description of a Meldrum continuous-grate destructor in successful operation for two months. See also editorial, p. 569.

1910

OPERATING results of the Seattle refuse destructor. 1800 w. (Engineering record. v. 62, p. 526.)   †† VDA

Sheerness, England.
See above, the General Works, under date of 1904.

Sheffield, England.

Serial

ANNUAL report of the cleansing department for the year ending March 25, 1900-1905, 1907-1911.
The cleansing department has charge of refuse removal, street cleaning, snow removal, public lavatories and public baths.

Special Cities — Sheffield, cont'd.
Non-serial
1903
DISPOSAL of a city's refuse. What Sheffield is doing. (Sanitary record. v. 32, p. 612.) † SPA

Shipley, England.
1903
SCHOFIELD, S. D. Destructor and electricity stations in small towns. 2300 w., 7 diagr. (Electrical engineer, London. v. 38, p. 808, 910.) †† VGA
Discussion 3000 w.
—— Same, abstract. 900 w. (Electrician, London. v. 52, p. 178.) †† VGA
With reference to the plant at Shipley, England.

Shoreditch, England.
See above, London.

Solingen, Germany.
1909
MÜLLABFUHR, Die, in Solingen. (Gesundheits-Ingenieur. Jahrg. 32, p. 803.) †† SPA

Somerville, Mass.
ANNUAL report of the board of health, 1878 (1st)-1911. (In: Somerville. Annual reports of the city.) *SYA
The collection of garbage, ashes and other refuse is under control of the board of health.

Southampton, England.
1888
BENNETT, William Benj. Geo. Southampton sewage clarification and house refuse disposal works. (Minutes of Proceedings Institution of Civil Engineers. v. 91, p. 310-313.) VDA

Southport, England.
1907
CONTINUOUS dust destructor (invented by the health superintendent of Southport). (Sanitary record. v. 39, p. 79.) † SPA

Southwark, England.
1908
CRUSHING house refuse. 1000 w. (Municipal journal and engineer. v. 24, p. 791.) †† SER
Borough of Southwark, Eng., crushes its mixed refuse, which can then be used as a fertilizer.
See also a note in County and municipal record. v. 10, p. 81. †† SPA

Stettin, Germany.
See above, the General Works, under date of 1908.

Stockholm, Sweden.
See also above, the General Works, under date of 1899.
1911
TINGSTEN, Karl. Stockholms renhållningsväsen från äldsta tider till våra dagar. Stockholm: P. A. Norstedt & Söner (1911). viii, 168 p. illus. pap. 4°.

Stuttgart, Germany.
1898
BUJARD, Alfons. Beseitigung städtischer Abfallstoffe (in Stuttgart). (Zeitschrift für Transportwesen und Strassenbau. v. 15, p. 104-106.) †† TPB

Sydney, New South Wales.
1903
RICHARDS, Richard Watkins. Notes upon municipal work in Sydney, N. S. W. (Minutes and Proceedings of the Institution of Civil Engineers. v. 152, p. 251-257.) VDA
Refuse disposal, p. 256-257.

Syracuse, N. Y.
See also above, the General Works, under date of 1908.
1900
GARBAGE disposal works, Syracuse, N. Y. 1,100 w., 2 drawings, 1 folding pl. (Engineering news. v. 44, p. 247.) †† VDA
Holthaus reduction system in use, by which fertilizers are made profitably.

Swansea, England.
1906
DESTRUCTEUR Horsfall à Swansea. (La Technique sanitaire. v. 1, p. 88-89.) † SPA
HORSFALL destructor at Swansea. (Sanitary record. v. 38, p. 51.) † SPA

Tacoma, Wash.
1895
HAWKS, A. McL. Garbage disposal at Tacoma and Seattle, Wash. 1400 w., 4 drawings. (Engineering news, v. 36, p. 21.) †† VDA

Taunton, Scotland.
1904
REFUSE destructor results for the twelve months ending Aug. 31, 1904. (County and municipal record. v. 4, p. 153.) † SPA

Toledo, O.
1905
TOLEDO garbage reduction plant. 1,800 w. (Bulletin of the League of American Municipalities. v. 3, p. 87.) †† SER
Garbage is digested with steam for eight hours and the grease extracted by cold naphtha.
1907
GARBAGE reduction process at Toledo. 900 w. (Engineering record. v. 56, p. 392.) †† VDA
Edison reduction process described. Plant was (1907) in the hands of receivers. See also letter, p. 608.

Toronto, Ont.
See also above, the General Works, under date of 1912.
1899
GARBAGE disposal at Toronto, Ont. 1,300 w., 2 drawings. 1899. (Engineering record. v. 40, p. 478.) †† VDA
Methods of collection of garbage, and cremators built.

Special Cities — Toronto, cont'd.

1900

JONES, John. An outline of the system of garbage collection in the city of Toronto. (Municipal engineering. v. 19, p. 392-394.) **VDA**
Mr. Jones writes as street commissioner of Toronto.

1903

JONES, John. The new garbage destructor at Toronto, Ont. (Municipal engineering. v. 25, p. 345-346.) **VDA**

1904

NEW garbage cremator at Toronto. (Engineering record. v. 50, p. 321-322.) †† **VDA**

1911

REPORT of methods of refuse disposal at Toronto. 2500 w. (Engineering record. Dec. 23, 1911.) †† **VDA**

1912

ECONOMIC study of the four alternate methods considered for the disposal of the garbage, rubbish and ashes of Toronto. 3500 w. (Engineering and contracting. March 27, 1912.) † **VDA**

Torquay, England.

1899

GARRETT, Henry A. Refuse disposal, and the results obtained from a six months' working of the refuse destructor at Torquay. (Engineering. v. 68, p. 215-216.) **VDA**

—— Same. (Proceedings Institution of Mechanical Engineers. v. 57, p. 419.) **VFA**

—— Same, abstract. 1400 w. (Engineering record. v. 40, p. 318.) †† **VDA**

—— Same, abstract and comment. 700 w.; discussion 3000 w. (Electrical review, London. v. 47, p. 238.) †† **VGA**

1902

DESTRUCTOR nuisance at Torquay. (Lancet. v. 162, p. 262-264; 335-336; 404-406.) **WAA**

Toulouse, France.

1909

GESCHWIND. Les rues de Toulouse au point de vue hygiénique. (Mémoires de l'Académie des sciences, inscriptions et belles-lettres de Toulouse. ser. 10, v. 9, p. 175-193.) * **EN**

Trenton, N. J.
See also above, the General Works, under date of 1908.

1903

HERING, Rudolph. Investigation of a garbage crematory. 7,500 w. (Scientific American supplement. v. 55, p. 22885, 22894.) †† **VA**

—— Same. (Engineering news. v. 48, p. 197.) †† **VDA**

1910

TRENTON, N. J. Health Board. Sanitary code, adopted Aug. 1, 1910. 89 p. 8°
Contains garbage removal regulations.

Twickenham, England.

NEW sewage works at Twickenham. illus. (Engineer. London, 1908. v. 105, p. 590-591, 630-632.) †† **VDA**

Vera Cruz, Mexico.

1902

IGLESIAS, Manuel S. Street hygiene in Vera Cruz and City of Mexico. (American Public Health Assoc. Public health papers and reports. v. 28, p. 75-77.) **SPA**

Vienna, Austria.
See also above, the General Works, under date of 1899.

1898

[TEXT of ordinance of Oct. 18, 1898, regulating the removal of ice and snow from sidewalks.] (Zeitschrift für Transportwesen und Strassenbau. v. 16, p. 61.) †† **TPB**

1900

HOFFMANN, Julius. Die Frage der Strassenhygiene in Wien. (Zeitschrift für Transportwesen und Strassenbau. v. 17, p. 51-53.) †† **TPB**
Abstract of a budget speech by the Gemeinde Rath Hoffmann.

1910

STREET cleaning in Vienna. 372 w. (Municipal journal and engineer. v. 29, p. 320.) †† **SER**

Vitry-sur-Seine, France.

1908

UTILISATION des ordures ménagères. 1300 w., 2 illus. (La nature. v. 70, p. 99.) **OA**
Description of new process at Vitry-sur-Seine, where the garbage is ground to a powder and oxidized, resulting powder being used as a fertilizer.

Walthamstowe, England.
See above, the General Works, under date of 1898.

Wandsworth, England.
See above, London.

Warrington, England.
See above, the General Works, under date of 1904.

Washington, D. C.

Serial

ANNUAL report on street and alley cleaning, 1888-1890. (In: D. C. Annual report of the health department, 1888-1890.) * **SBK**
Continued as:
ANNUAL report of the superintendent of street and alley cleaning, 1890 (1st)-1911. (In: D. C. Annual report of the commissioners, 1890-1911.) * **SBK**
On Feb. 6, 1888, the supervision of the service of street, avenue and alley cleaning was transferred from the engineer department of the D. C. to the health department and so remained to Sept. 15, 1889, when it was transferred to the police department, until Sept. 30, 1890, when the street and alley service was made a separate and independent branch of the public service.
A synopsis of the report for 1900 is printed in Municipal engineering. v. 19, p. 233-234. **VDA**

Special Cities — Washington, cont'd.

Non-serial
1895

GARBAGE contract concluded Sept. 4, 1895; text. (D. C. Annual report of the commissioners. 1896, p. 1169-1173.)   *SBK

WOODWARD, William C. Report relative to investigation of the methods of garbage disposal in Philadelphia and Wilmington, Del. [also Atlanta, Ga., Allegheny, Pittsburgh, Cincinnati, St. Louis, Camden, N. J., and Blissville, L. I.] (D. C. Annual report of the commissioners. 1896, p. 1174-1188.)   *SBK

1896

LETTER from the commissioners of the District of Columbia making full report of their action under Act of March 2, 1895, in the matter of the removal of the garbage of the cities of Washington and Georgetown. 8 p. 8°. (U. S. 54 cong., 1 sess., Senate doc. 220, v. 8.)   *SBE

PROPOSAL for the incineration of general refuse for a period of four years, beginning July 1 1896. (D C. Annual report of the commissioners 1896, p. 1189-1192.)   *SBK

1900

COLLECTION and disposal of garbage, etc., D. C. Report of the Committee on the District of Columbia. 3 p. 8°. (U. S. 56 cong., 1 sess., Senate doc. 338, v. 2.)   *SBE

1901

WOODWARD, William C. Refuse disposal in the District of Columbia. (American Public Health Assoc. Public health papers and reports. v. 27, p. 194-203.)   SPA

—— Same, extracts. (Engineering record. v. 44, p. 301.)   ††VDA

1903

CLEANING asphalt streets by flushing in [Washington, D. C.]. (Municipal engineering. v. 25, p. 259.)   VDA

STREET cleaning methods in Washington, D. C. (Same. v. 25, p. 260-261.)   VDA

1906

See above Rochester, N. Y., this date.

1907

COST of street cleaning in Washington. (Municipal engineering. v. 33, p. 260-261.)   VDA

1908

STREET cleaning [especially as it relates to Washington]. (Municipal engineering. v. 34, p. 184.)   VDA

Watford, England.
See also above, the General Works, under date of 1904.

1904

WATFORD's new dust destructor. (Sanitary record. v. 33, p. 318-319.)   †SPA

West Hartlepool, England.
See also above, the General Works, under dates of 1901 and 1904.

1904

BROWN, J. W. West Hartlepool refuse destructor. (Sanitary record. v. 33, p. 399-401.)   †SPA

Westmount, Quebec.
1906

COMBINED municipal refuse destructor and electric generating station. 1,200 w., 3 illus. (Engineering record. v. 54, p. 186.)   ††VDA

ELECTRIC lighting without coal; the Meldrum destructor at Westmount, Canada. 2,500 w. (Municipal journal and engineer. v. 20, p. 453.)   ††SER
Successful results obtained from combined disposal and electric-lighting plant.

FELLOWS, F. C. Westmount, Quebec, garbage destructor. (Municipal engineering. v. 31, p. 50-53.)   VDA

MÜLL-VERBRENNUNGSANLAGE nebst Elektrizitätswerk in Westmount. (Zeitschrift für Transportwesen und Strassenbau. Jahrg. 23, p. 387-388; illus.)   ††TPB

REFUSE destructor combined with electric light plant at Westmount, P. Q. 3,000 w., 1 diagr., 4 drawings, 4 illus. (Engineering news. v. 55, p. 586.)   ††VDA
Includes an eight-hour test of the burning and evaporative powers of the Meldrum destructor. See also editorial, p. 583.

1910

DISPOSAL of city refuse. 5000 w. (Canadian engineer. Aug. 25, 1910.)   ††VDA
General methods adopted in Canada, illustrating Westmount incinerating plant.

THOMPSON, George W. Westmount incinerator and power plant. 2500 w. (Canadian electrical news. July, 1910.)   ††VGA

Wheeling, W. Va.
1886

BAIRD, George. Destruction of night-soil and garbage by fire. (American Public Health Assoc. Public health papers and reports. v. 12, p. 119-122; Sanitary engineer. v. 15, p. 20.)   SPA
Describes successful experiments at Wheeling with a Smith gas-furnace.

1911

OFFICIAL test of the Decarie garbage and refuse incinerator at Wheeling, W. Va. (Municipal engineering. v. 40, p. 460.)   VDA

Wiesbaden, Germany.
See also above, the General Works, under the dates of 1908 and 1909.

1906

BERLITT, B. Der Bau der Kehrichtverbrennungs-anstalt in Wiesbaden. (Gesundheits-Ingenieur. Jahrg. 29, p. 537-544.)   †SPA

—— Same, reviewed. (Revue d'hygiène publique et de police sanitaire. v. 29, p. 1126-1127.)   SPA

MÜLLVERBRENNUNGSANLAGE mit Dörrschen Ofen der Stadt Wiesbaden. (Zeitschrift des Vereins Deutscher Ingenieure. Bd. 50, p. 1641-1642.)   VDA

Special Cities, cont'd.

Windsor, England.

1904

A dust [i. e. refuse] destructor for Windsor. (County and municipal record. v. 3, p. 55.)   **SPA**
Hearing on application of town council of Windsor for power to contract a loan to erect a refuse destructor.

Winnipeg, Manitoba.

1907

Testing a garbage cremator.   250 w. (In Municipal journal and engineer. v. 23, p. 191.)   †† **SER**
Conditions for proposed test of a Decarie incinerator at Winnipeg, Canada.

Withington, England.

1903

Withington new refuse destructor. (Sanitary record. v. 31, p. 39-40.)   † **SPA**

Worcester, Mass.

Annual report of the board of health, 1878 (1st) – 1893. (In: Worcester. City documents. 1879-1894.)   * **SYA**
Contains reports of the scavenger department on garbage and refuse collection and removal. No reports seem to be made after 1893.

Annual report of the commissioner of highways, 1864-1893. (In: Worcester. City documents, 1865-1894.)   * **SYA**

Continued as:

Annual report of the commissioner of streets, 1894-1911. (In: Same, 1895-1912.)   * **SYA**

York, Pa.

1908

York's [Pa.] garbage reduction plant. 800 w. (Municipal journal and engineer. v. 25, p. 217.)   †† **SER**

Zürich, Switzerland.
See also above, the General Works, under date of 1907.

1896

Mettler, R., and H. Staub. Verbrennungsanlagen für Haus- und Strassenkehricht. (Zeitschrift für Transportwesen und Strassenbau. v. 13, p. 346-348, 365-366, 381-383, 398-399, 413-414, 432-434, 452-453.)   †† **TPB**
Feasibility of various destructors for Zürich.

S., A. Verbrennungs-Anlagen für Haus- und Strassenkehricht. (Same. v. 13, p. 256-257.)   †† **TPB**
An essay on the report by Mettler and Staub.

1902

Kehrichtverbrennungs-Anstalt in Zürich. (Zeitschrift für Transportwesen und Strassenbau. v. 19, p. 429-430.)   †† **TPB**

1904

Gradenwitz, Alfred.   Steam turbine in a refuse destruction plant.   1000 w. (Municipal engineering. v. 27, p. 409.)   **VDA**
Horsfall destructors at Zürich generate steam for a 220 h. p. Brown-Boveri-Parsons turbine.

1905

Combustion des ordures ménagères à Zürich. (Annales d'hygiène publique. ser. 4, v. 5, p. 182-183.)   **SPA**
—— Same. (L'electricien. ser. 2, v. 3, p. 96.)   †† **VGA**

CONCLUSION